To Mother

Christmas 1975.

GW00715459

With all our love

Esmé and Bill.

SUSSEX

1   *Frontispiece (overleaf) Rye, as seen by a quarter-boy*

JOHN BURKE

SUSSEX

B. T. Batsford Ltd
London

For MY MOTHER
who had the good taste to ensure my being
born in the right town in the right county

and UNCLE WILL
who has the good sense to be there still

First published 1974

© John Burke 1974

ISBN 0 7134 2814 7

Printed and bound in Great Britain by Cox & Wyman Ltd,
London, Fakenham and Reading for the publishers B. T.
Batsford Ltd, 4 Fitzhardinge Street, London W1H 0AH

CONTENTS

ACKNOWLEDGMENTS

The Author wishes to thank those friends and acquaintances, too many to name, and the many passing strangers who by a word here and a comment there have helped him on his way. He is especially grateful to Bruce Hudson, James Lister and Godfrey Harding; to Bill Malia and Roger Weekes of Horsham; to Bill Sellick of Mayfield; and to Charles Shippam of Boxgrove, who steered him in what might be called a dozen different directions at once were this not to give a misleading impression of something rather painful, which is the exact opposite of the truth. None of them should, however, be blamed for any errors of fact or waywardness of opinion expressed in the ensuing pages.

The Author and Publishers wish to thank the following for permission to reproduce the illustrations appearing in this book: J. Allan Cash (Pls 20, 24, 25); Noel Habgood (Pls 4, 8, 13, 14, 26, 27); A. F. Kersting (Pls 6, 7, 9, 11, 17, 21, 22, 23); Eric de Mare (Frontispiece, 12, 19); Kenneth Scowen (Pls 16); the late Edwin Smith (Pls 3, 5, 10, 15, 18).

The map is by Patrick Leeson.

THE ILLUSTRATIONS

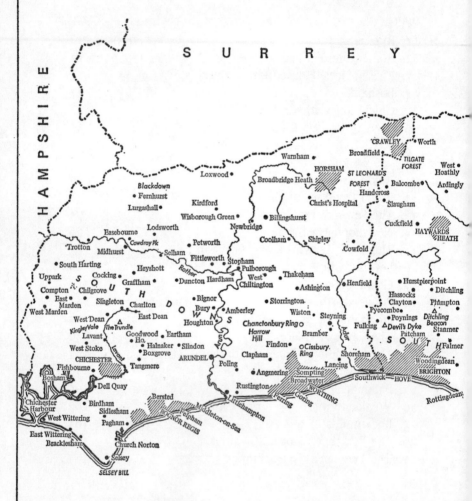

CHAPTER ONE

Invaders

Set in the wall beside the entrance to Chichester's Council
House and Assembly Room is a stone dug up from a near-by
corner in 1723. Its Latin inscription dedicates a temple to
Neptune and Minerva on behalf of the safety of the Roman
imperial house, 'by the authority of Tiberius Claudius
Cogidubnus, King and Legate of Augustus in Britain'.

At the far end of the county, modern Normans have
set up – perhaps in a spirit of mild remorse – a small monument in the grounds of Battle Abbey, commemorating
the spot where their ancestors defeated and slew Saxon
Harold.

These memorials recall what were assuredly the two
most successful and significant full-scale invasions of
England by way of its vulnerable south-east coast. The
Romans' arrival near Chichester was apparently unopposed,
unlike the legions' assault upon Kent; but the battle of
Saxons and Normans on Senlac Hill was bloody and un-
sparing. Between the two extremes and, indeed, between
the two places there has over the centuries been many
another infiltration, head-on attack, and threat of attack
along shores so dangerously close to the Continent. Coast
and countryside, like the people themselves, are a mixture
of conflicting elements and recollections, gradually fused
into improbable harmony. Across Sussex lie layer upon
layer of prehistoric relics, Roman roads and villas, Saxon
and Danish names, Norman walls and Norman laws. And
there are castles, towers, waterways and overgrown
defences against invasions which never came. Here is enough
to keep the archæologist or historian happy for a lifetime.

I was born in Sussex. Too much of my life has been spent

away from it, and every now and then I feel a touch of that dread expressed by Hilaire Belloc for the moment when 'by some evil fortune a Sussex man dies far away from home'. Like Belloc, too, I retain a stubbornly romantic belief that on Judgment Day, when less blessed counties are engulfed by a horrible great rain of fire, this rain will fall on Appledore but not on Rye.

Stubborn, yes: whatever the varying blends of inherited characteristics and whatever the pressures of past and present, our competitors and enemies will dourly confirm the truth of our boast – 'I'm a Sussex pig, and I won't be druv'. Coaxed and cajoled, possibly; driven, never.

When friends say that Sussex has been ruined, that invaders from inland have despoiled it far more savagely than invaders from the sea ever did, I nod agreement. We lament that most of it is just commuter country or a tourists' amusement arcade. Old family businesses in Rye have become olde-worlde tea shoppes; Alfriston is a coarsened, over-amplified pop star; there is no pleasure in walking along the rural lanes we once knew, because cars are for ever driving us into the hedge . . . and beyond that hedge is a caravan park. The coastline is beyond redemption, having flagrantly defied the warning of the wise Isaiah: 'Woe unto them that join house to house, that lay field to field, till there be no place'.

Yet within a few hours of being home (for of course it will always be home, even if I were never to see it again) I know that all this is nonsense. It may be true on the surface, just as it is true that the A.285 and A.29 are busy, noisy, often intolerably congested roads; but for much of their way they rest on Stane Street, the great Roman thoroughfare from Chichester to London. True, also, that Peacehaven offers no peace to anyone whose eyes, ears and nose are in reasonable working order; but immediately behind it are the still magnificent Downs, the ancient pastures and the tumuli, here long before the bungalows and destined to out-live them. The surface is only a veneer. All that is best in the past is, with a loving eye, clearly discernible through it. As for what is best in the present : half a mile off any main road is the village you thought no longer existed, half an hour's determined climb up a scarp of the South Downs will reveal the same vision the Celts, the Romans and your grandfather knew, and Kipling's 'little, lost, Down churches' still offer up their praise. To list the secluded, welcoming, traditional inns of the region would be to give the impression that the author of this book is a raging alcoholic.

The county of Sussex is about 75 miles long, and nowhere more than 28 miles from north to south, producing a total area of 1,457 square miles. Its outline, appropriately enough when one hears farmers grumbling of the great flints which 'grow' out of its chalk uplands, is like that of a flint axe, narrowing to a jagged cutting edge in the east. The Normans divided it into six administrative districts, largely conditioned by the site facilities for ports and fortresses commanding the main harbours and rivers – the Lavant, Arun, Adur and Ouse, with the eastern Rother and the Kent Ditch raggedly sketching in an eastern border. Today there are two administrative areas : West Sussex, with its offices in Chichester, and the larger area of East Sussex based on Lewes. But these vertical slices were and are purely jurisdictional, the earlier on a military framework, the contemporary for civil purposes. The natural geological divisions are fourfold and horizontal, running in rough parallel from west to east.

In the extreme south is the coastal plain, narrowing and for a spell squeezed out of existence where the South Downs reach the sea. These Downs form the next swathe, running east-south-east from Hampshire to Beachy Head. Below their northern slopes are the Vale of Sussex and the Weald, and rising beyond, where Sussex gives way to west Kent and Surrey, is the Forest Ridge of greensand hills.

When much of this shifting coast lay below the sea, something approximating to our present Sussex must have been a large island of chalk. By the time of the last Ice Age it was joined to the mainland, and as the ice receded and burgeoning rivers sought a way out of the northern ridge, the centre of the plateau was gradually eroded. Some streams were lost in the porous limestone, but others carved their channels to the sea and relentlessly chewed at the surrounding rock. There remained chalk hills around the rim, but within the scooped-out bowl appeared the sands, sandstones and clay, some fertile and some freakishly sterile, of what came to be known as the Weald.

The name appears early in the *Anglo-Saxon Chronicle* as *Andredes leag* and in later forms such as *Andredes wald* or *Andredsweald*. All of these can mean, more or less, a wood or large tract of land belonging to Andred, and on the face of it there seems a connection with the Roman fortress of Anderida, at what is now Pevensey. Many scholars, however, point to the frequent use of the word 'weald' to denote waste land, and the spelling 'wild' was often adopted. There is good reason to favour the translation, 'the wilderness where nobody dwells'.

Certainly this would for centuries have been an appropriate description. A vast, impenetrable forest had grown up within the eroded basin, and neither the skilled Romans nor their barbarian successors ventured far into it. Yet there were great natural resources there, as earlier arrivals in this country had discovered.

The first men to reach our shores were Old Stone Age hunters during a lull in the Ice Age, possibly as much as half a million years ago. Increasing cold drove them back to more temperate climes, leaving behind a few flint tools

2 *Roman mosaic, Fishbourne*

as mementoes of their fragile tenure. When the climate improved and while England was still joined to the Continental land mass, Middle Stone Age hunters retraced the steps of their ancestors and continued to pursue game with arrows and spears tipped with flint, remnants of which have been dug up or found in old trackways in many parts of Sussex.

When the causeway linking this country to the Continent was finally inundated, warmer currents in the surrounding seas encouraged a spread of vegetation, including the woodlands of the coast and the Weald. At the same time the nomadic hunters were learning the arts of animal husbandry and primitive agriculture, and the advantages of co-operation rather than rivalry with their fellows. By New Stone Age, or Neolithic, times, communities were forming within causewayed camps. These hill forts started with a simple protective bank and ditch, but in time grew more imposing, with parallel sequences of ramparts, and wooden defences across the entrances. Some were so huge that they could hardly have been permanent settlements, but may have served as religious meeting places or as a refuge for several friendly communities threatened by less friendly newcomers. These settlers did not just live together, but lay together in death, in long barrows sealed off, when full, with stone or earth.

Well-finished stone axes replaced the weapons of the huntsman, not so much for warfare as for clearing woodland and making timber defences for the camps.

Like their predecessors, the new communities relied on flint for tools and weapons. Mine shafts were dug into the chalk, often as deep as 50 feet, with picks of bone or deer antlers. Today these clusters of shafts, such as those on Harrow Hill and others in the vicinity of Worthing, show on the surface as groups of irregular hollows and hummocks. Below ground, the roofs of some old workings

3   *The Novices' House, Battle Abbey*

are still stained by the smoke of ancient lamps using animal fat.

A new wave of immigrants from the Mediterranean sought copper and tin for the manufacture of bronze. They were known as the Beaker Folk because their dead, buried in individual rather than communal graves, were ritually accompanied by a decorated, flat-bottomed drinking vessel. In due course cremation became more common, the urns being buried in bell-shaped tumuli or sunken 'pond' barrows. There are hundreds of such cemeteries across Sussex, mainly on the Downs. One of the most impressive is on Bow Hill near Chilgrove, a region rich in earthworks of many different periods, and also boasting flint mines in Lavant caves. In the 1960s an impressive burial ground marked by circles of huge stones was found between Crawley and Horsham, but after study had unfortunately to be abandoned to the demands of agriculture.

Between 600 and 400 B.C. the Bronze Age settlers were threatened by new incursions from the Continent. The belligerent Celts ushered in the Iron Age and scattered or subdued the resident farmers and traders.

The sandstone of the Weald had rich veins of iron ore. Although successive races of invaders seem to have been scared of the dark forest and reluctant to exploit more than its extreme fringes, the Celts must have made some attempt to extract a mineral so valuable to them. There is evidence of tree clearance in parts of Ashdown Forest around what may well have been mining camps, and by the time the Romans came there was a long tradition of iron working in the region.

The Celts also introduced new farming methods. They brought with them ploughs drawn by oxen in place of the foot-plough hitherto used, and the remaining traces of their settlement near Plumpton show the earliest examples in this country of lynchets. These rectangular Celtic fields

4 Bosham

are generally about 400 feet by 100 feet, utterly different from the pinched, haphazard plots of Bronze Age farmers. Their detection became easier with the invention of aerial photography, which clearly shows up the ridges and extent of the original fields. More than a quarter of the downland between the Adur and the Ouse shows signs of them; there is a recognisable pattern on Windover Hill, near Eastbourne; and several were laid out within the ramparts of Cissbury Ring.

Cissbury was one of the many hill forts taken over and strengthened by the newcomers. They added massive new ramparts to the Trundle – now a favourite parking and picnic site near Goodwood race-course – and developed combined villages and fortifications such as that on Mount Caburn near Lewes, which remained of importance until well into Roman times.

The Barbican House Museum in Lewes has a fine collection of finds from Caburn and other sites, including flint and bronze implements, restored pottery vessels, cinerary urns, and ornaments of different ages. Brighton Museum also has material from various periods and places: the bones of a mother and child from the fortified camp now obliterated by the race-course, more implements and weapons, and one very special treasure – a magnificent bowl hollowed from a single block of amber, probably brought from Scandinavia by some powerful chieftain.

* * *

The renewal of old fortifications and the establishment of new ones may have been spurred on by the influx of even more warlike tribes into Britain. The Belgae, seeking refuge from Roman harassment, did not in fact penetrate far into Sussex, but there was no assurance that they might not eventually make the attempt. For a while, however, they preferred to consolidate their gains in Kent and to offer

5   *Chichester Cathedral*

such help as they could to kinsmen still on the Continent struggling against Rome.

In 55 B.C. Julius Caesar decided to deal with this problem. He landed in Kent but failed to establish a bridgehead. The following year he came back, defeated the most powerful of the south-eastern leaders, and exacted guarantees of regular tribute to follow. The campaign had been little more than a gesture, and during the next hundred years the only Romans visiting Britain were peaceful traders.

Sussex had escaped most of these troubles. But four years after Caesar's withdrawal a direct assault was launched on the Selsey peninsula by another Belgic tribe, the Atrebates. This could be directly attributed to Caesar's own activities. Back on the Continent he had found himself engaged in the suppression of continual tribal uprisings against Roman rule, among them a revolt by Commius, king of the Atrebates, hitherto a wary ally of Rome. Faced with defeat, Commius and some of his leading warriors fled across the seas to the mouth of what is now Chichester Harbour. They set about subjugating all the neighbouring tribes, until they dominated most of West Sussex, Surrey, Hampshire and Berkshire.

After the death of Commius his three sons shared out his conquests. As with so many legacies then and now, they were soon quarrelling among themselves. Before being dispossessed by one of his brothers, however, Tincommius was master of West Sussex for long enough to create a prosperous trading centre near his people's original landing-place. It was not so long since they had been at war with the Romans, but business was business, and the Atrebates opened up amicable trade relations with their ex-enemy from the town which was to become known as Regnum, later Noviomagus, and ultimately Chichester.

Plenty of evidence of this commercial prosperity has been found over the years. Coins, pottery and jewellery continue to turn up on the shores around Selsey and the Witterings, and surviving Roman records speak of trade in gold, silver, iron, skins and other commodities.

The most impressive record of all is one which poses as many questions as it answers on the Romano–British relationship at a time when peaceful commerce had to give way to armed conflict.

During the laying of a water main in 1960 in Fishbourne, a village which is in effect a pleasant little suburb of Chichester, a workman came upon some rubble obviously belonging to a much earlier century. When his employer reported it to the local archaeological society, they soon discovered that below the field was a late first-century building, and below that traces of something even earlier. Fishbourne had already yielded fragments of mosaic and masonry from what must have been the edge of the old Roman harbour, but nothing of this magnitude.

Eight years of careful excavation revealed the outlines of a palace which could originally have been as extensive as Nero's in Rome. Much has since been lost under a housing estate and the main Portsmouth road; but what is left, now sheltered by modern glass and roofing, conjures up the lavish life style of some enormously influential functionary. Everything points to the favoured Tiberius Claudius Cogidubnus, the Briton with a Romanised name and the appointment, as we have seen on the Minerva stone, of imperial King and Legate in Britain.

Why should one native chieftain be accorded such distinction? And another question: was he here when the Romans invaded in A.D. 43 – was he a party, perhaps, to the invitation to them to invade – or did he come with them? There are several theories, and several certainties.

For some time the Atrebates, like other southern communities, had been threatened by the growing power of the Belgic king Cunobelinus (Shakespeare's Cymbeline) who from his capital at Camulodunum (Colchester) was greedy for more territory. When he died and his sons squabbled over their inheritance, many of the tribes who had suffered at their hands seized the moment for revolt. King Cogidubnus of the Regni was one who decided it was time to strike back.

It is known that refugees from Britain in Rome had been appealing to the Emperor Claudius to come to the aid of their countrymen. Among them was one of Cunobelinus's sons who had been forced to flee from his brothers. There is also a story that Cogidubnus himself had fled to Rome and added his voice to those pleas; but other sources claim that he remained in his capital and merely sent urgent messages to Rome.

When Claudius decided to mount his invasion in A.D. 43, his commander, Aulus Plautius, concentrated on a landing near what is now Richborough in Kent. There is a long-standing belief in the Manhood area between Chichester and Selsey that a subsidiary landing was made at West Wittering. This is hotly contested by most experts, yet one cannot help toying with the idea. If Cogidubnus really was in Rome and returned with the invading forces, he would have been eager to re-establish himself in his homeland, preferably with at least a token contingent of his Roman friends to show rivals that he meant to hold what was his. If not, and he was maintaining a defiant resistance there until his call for help was answered, it would have been politic for the liberators to send such a contingent to ease the pressure and show that the call had indeed been answered.

Certainly, then or immediately afterwards, they must have regarded this 'client king' as a valuable ally. Throughout the rest of Britain for the next 40 years the legions steadily eliminated all opposition, until at last the sons of defeated chieftains and useful businessmen could be trusted to adopt Roman ways and take over day-to-day administration according to Roman regulations. But right from the start Cogidubnus, though apparently of much less military consequence than many a northern chieftain, was honoured almost as an equal. Even if landings were not made here early in the campaign, Vespasian, the general who was later to become emperor, undoubtedly used the port and harbour as headquarters for operations to the west. Land was given to Cogidubnus, and his people were accorded the privilege of being treated as *socii*, or allies, of Rome.

A conjectural reconstruction of the palace at Fishbourne shows it with enclosed gardens, a spacious courtyard, regal apartments, bath houses, an audience chamber, monumental colonnades, and a sumptuous guest wing. The excavations reveal a highly efficient central heating system, tessellated corridors, bath, a frigidarium, and a wealth of mosaic floors throughout. Only fragments remain of many of these designs, but happily there are also a few nearly complete, including a beautiful design of a cupid riding a dolphin in a surround of fabulous sea beasts, and one in which a blend of geometrical motifs plays cunning tricks on the eye of the beholder. Pollen analysis and meticulous research have made possible the reconstruction of the courtyard and the replanting of species whose remains were identified in the soil. A pattern of narrow trenches delineated the walks, hedges and general proportions of the gardens; ceramic water-mains flanked the paths; and the remains of some marble basins indicate the extent of the system of fountains.

When this pampered King and Legate died he seems to have left no heir. Perhaps his usefulness to the Romans was over, for they set up no important figure in his place, but allowed the palace to be split up into what one is tempted to call luxury flats with all mod cons. In A.D. 270 the glory departed: fire raged through the buildings, which were never restored and never inhabited again.

Whether with their own resources or with the aid of their trusted legate, the Romans set about developing Noviomagus into a form still identifiable in modern Chichester, with four main roads leaving the centre at right angles and passing through gates in the surrounding wall. As at Fishbourne, testimonies to their handiwork keep reappearing. In 1935 an amphitheatre was discovered but built over and lost, to await joyful re-discovery by some lucky future excavator. A forum and basilica lie beneath the cathedral. In 1972 an architect watching the sinking of boreholes for foundations of new buildings on Eastgate Square noticed that the mechanical digger was beginning to throw up an odd mixture of sandstone and mortar. Chichester Civic Society's director of excavations was hastily summoned and, with the commendably selfless co-operation of the site owners and their architect, excavation began on what proved to be a fourth-century Roman bastion. It was probably the original Eastgate, guarding the entrance to the city of the most famous of all Roman roads in this region – Stane Street.

This 57-mile highway was one of the key routes of the south, linking Noviomagus and its busy harbour with London via Pulborough and Alfoldean. At intervals there were posting stations, and narrower branch roads served the needs of adjacent agricultural communities. Stane Street crossed the river Arun by a stone and wood bridge, fragments of which came to light about 40 years ago during a drought, and continued its way through Dorking and Merton towards Londinium.

It was only to be expected that wealthy Romans and Romanised Britons would build country villas for themselves not too far from the line of such a road, and some have been unearthed in the Pulborough and Wiggonholt area. They were not simply holiday homes or week-end cottages, but in most cases formed the centre of a farm or ranch, with accommodation for servants, labourers and skilled craftsmen.

The best-preserved remains are those of Bignor, beautifully situated on a gentle slope facing the Downs, some ten miles north-east of Chichester. This time it was a plough which was responsible for discovery of the site. In July 1811 it struck a large stone, below which was a mosaic of Ganymede and accompanying dancers. George Tupper, owner of the land, and John Hawkins of Bignor Park spent the next eight years painstakingly digging, sifting and clearing. They gradually exposed the basis of an extremely large residence which must have been expanded between the second and fourth century, echoing the expansion of the original farm into a profitable sheep ranch. There were spacious living rooms, bathrooms, and central heating. Until 1956 there was much speculation about the source of water for all this, but then water-pipe trenches were found beside the villa and running north towards a stream bed from which supplies were probably drawn.

The first mosaic floor to be uncovered was not the only one. In time there came to the surface a Medusa with writhing locks, an almost intact geometrical mosaic, and a bleak head of Winter in what must once have been a spacious representation of the Seasons. Loveliest of all is the brooding, sensual, blue-haloed Venus accompanied by, yet utterly aloof from, a panel of podgy gladiators oddly personified as cupids.

All the rooms and passages so far excavated have been protected by hunts of flint and thatch, giving from a distance the impression of an African kraal.

With them the Romans brought not only their skills in road-making and defence works but also the crafts of the pottery and glass maker, and of the iron-worker. In view of their dependence on this metal it is surprising that they did not attack the rich resources of *Silva Anderida*, the Weald, more vigorously. Ivan Margary's masterly research has proved the existence of far more extensive Roman ways in the Weald than had hitherto been suspected by most pundits; yet there was not the large-scale exploitation of the iron ore which the Romans could surely have achieved. Like earlier colonists they seemed happier on the perimeter of the forest than in its uncharted depths. In 1972 a battery of over 30 Romano–British furnaces, each about two feet in diameter, was discovered at Broadfield, near Crawley, on the northern fringe of the Weald. Furnaces have been identified at Sedlescombe and Westfield to the east. The metalling of Roman roads often contains a great deal of slag, as in the one from Edenbridge to Maresfield, presumably taken from ironworks not too far from the route. In the nineteenth century huge mounds of such slag in Beauport Park, near Battle, were broken up for just such a purpose.

Still the primeval forest was not ready to surrender all its wealth. It was not until the Middle Ages that its systematic ravishment began.

The Romans stayed in Britain for about 400 years, by the end of which time they were being harried from the north by Picts and Scots, and from the east and south by Angles and Saxons, while Rome itself was in such peril from barbarians that fighting men from all over the empire were having to be recalled to defend the homeland.

When some attempt was still being made to retain a grip on Britain, a Count of the Saxon Shore was appointed with the unenviable task of constructing and holding a coastal defence system from the Wash round to Southampton. Many minor fortresses set up by the rebel Carausius, who had for a time challenged Roman hegemony, were adapted and strengthened. Signal stations were equipped to send out warnings of impending attack. Harbour defences were hurriedly and, one imagines, sketchily reinforced and manned by the depleted and disheartened levies still remaining.

In Sussex, what we now know as Pevensey was the isolated fort of Anderida, guarding a wide harbour. Its solid walls, 12 feet thick, were bound together by a tough cement which still endures. The uneven contour, adapted to the hillock on which it stands, bulges with great drum-towers. In due course the Normans were to find it a useful starter for a castle of their own. The sea receded long ago, but the massive defences were still fit for use during the Second World War, when a pill-box and machine-gun emplacement were incorporated.

Anderida did not, however, fulfil its supposed function of deterring the Saxons.

Once the legions had departed, leaving Britain to cope as well as it might with these new enemies, sporadic raids turned into calculated campaigns. In Kent the misguided Vortigern, ruler of territories stretching as far away as South Wales, invited two Jutish chieftains to help him against the Picts in return for grants of land. These two, Hengist and Horsa, honoured the bargain for as long as it suited them and then, the ranks of their mercenaries swollen by opportunists from their native Rhineland, turned on their hosts and butchered them. Those who surrendered, wrote the Venerable Bede, 'were doomed to lifelong servitude even if not massacred on the spot'.

Sussex, its borders protected by inhospitable marsh and forest, did not at first feel the full impact. Then in A.D. 477 the Saxons landed in force.

*   *   *

According to the *Anglo-Saxon Chronicle*, 'Aella came to Britain with his three sons Cymen, Wlencing and Cissa in three ships at the place which is called Cymenesora, and there slew many Wealas, and drove some in flight into the wood which is called Andredes leag'.

The place called Cymenesora, or Cymen's Shore, is close to that tip of the Selsey peninsula where the Atrebates had disembarked 500 years before. From here the first objective was Noviomagus, sinking into dereliction since its abandonment by the Romans, but still a place of some size. It was later rebuilt by Cissa, Aella's third son, so becoming Cissan-ceaster (in some later documents Cicestria), not so much meaning 'Cissa's castle' as 'Cissa's old fortifications', making it clear that this was something taken over rather than created – perhaps most aptly phrased by W. E. P. Done as 'the old fortress at Cissa's place'. He may also have given his name to Cissbury, 'Cissa's fort'.

The Wealas referred to appear elsewhere as Wales, both names being simply versions of the Anglo-Saxon word for aliens, applied indiscriminately to all the native Britons they met. Driven remorselessly westward, their survivors became the Welsh, their country Wales.

The Saxons themselves were probably named after the *seax*, the single-edged short sword which was their most feared weapon. With it they began to carve their way across the countryside, though by our standards their progress seems, looking back, to have been fairly slow. It took Aella over 13 years to reach and storm Anderida or Andredesceaster, where, despite the Britons' skill in 'beating the besiegers in the day by stratagems and in the night by attacks', every last one was put to the sword. Presumably each outward thrust from the first landing at Cymenesora was consolidated by new arrivals and by treaties with those of the conquered whose lives were spared, before a further step was taken.

Much more time elapsed before the county names as we know them settled into recognisable form. This is hardly surprising in view of the precariousness of their boundaries:

the Angle and Saxon petty kingdoms fought each other as greedily as they had fought the Britons, and although we tidily assert today that Essex was the land of the East Saxons, Middlesex of the Middle Saxons, Wessex of the West Saxons and Sussex of the South Saxons, the divisions were never quite so clear cut. Wessex, paradoxically the one which is no longer with us save in the novels of Thomas Hardy, was continually gobbling up neighbours or pressuring them to form alliances under its leadership, until by the time of Egbert it effectively dominated most of England.

The South Saxons rarely enjoyed more than a shaky independence. Yet, as with peoples of occupied or threatened countries whose awareness of national identity grows stronger with each new humiliation, their county name began to emerge just at the time of their integration into a larger entity. The *Anglo-Saxon Chronicle* gives it as Suthseaxe, which in itself just means the South Saxons, and references continue to 'the land of the Suthseaxe' until the word becomes the regional name and eventually solidifies into Sussex.

Even so it did not originally define the county as we now understand it. Between the South Saxons and the Jutes of Kent there existed for some time a separate people, followers of a Saxon or Danish adventurer called Haesten or Haesta, who gave his name to the settlement of Hastings.

Following the example of Cissa's transformation of Noviomagus into Chichester, one might expect to find other strongholds, well-planned townships and desirable residences adapted by the victorious invaders to their own use. Instead, they allowed old forts to crumble, and built none of their own. They did not even bother to keep the roads in repair.

None of the Saxons, as Tacitus had observed of their forebears, cared for urban life, 'and they do not even tolerate houses built in rows. They dwell apart and at a distance from each other, according to the preference they may have for the stream, the plain, or the grove. They make no use of stone cut from the quarry, or of tiles; for every sort of building they use unshapely wood . . .' Like gypsies mistrustful of settled homesteads, they fought shy of anything left behind by their predecessors, whether it be a hill-top earthwork or an attractively sited Roman villa.

It was true, of course, that many a noble building had already been allowed to decay. In the twilight of Romanised Britain, the peoples left behind by the Romans had themselves lost heart and, apparently, lost all will to maintain the civilised accoutrements of the way of life they had been taught. Whole towns were abandoned. The luxurious villas stood exposed to wind and rain, while the Saxon newcomers contented themselves with building shacks of wood and mud for their farms and skimpy villages, their 'tuns' (enclosures) and 'dens' (forest clearings). The burnt-out ruins of the palace at Fishbourne were overlaid by fields, and if a plough cut through an occasional wall or turned up a few fragments of mosaic, this was regarded only as an irritating interruption of the steady rhythm of the task.

Liking neither the uplands with their tumuli and ghosts, nor the relics of forgotten Rome, the Saxons tended to settle at the foot of the Downs, facing south to the sea or north to the Weald, where water was plentiful and the land easy to cultivate. They made tentative advances into the forest, making clearings for pasturing their swine; but ignored the iron resources of the Weald, and did nothing to rebuild such abandoned furnaces as they came across.

There are, naturally, few traces anywhere of the wooden dwellings of the Saxons. But wandering through Sussex we do find, at last, some attempt at permanence. With the return of Christianity came a vigorous spell of church building, much of it still in wood, but also much in stone. Doors, arches and pilasters survive in structures which have been adapted and restored in later centuries. Repair and rebuilding operations often bring to light sturdy Saxon foundations. And there are a few almost complete, unspoilt examples. In Bishopstone, named after the bishops of Selsey to whom it belonged, the flint church of St Andrew dates from between 900 and 950. It has a fine, square, uncompromising tower and a high Saxon porch, over which is a sundial with the name of Ead-ric carved into it. Much farther north, near Crawley, the largest Saxon church in England is to be found at Worth. It appears to have been built according to specifications laid down by Alfred the Great, though not started until half a century after his death. Alfred decreed that Roman buildings still surviving should be neglected no longer, but repaired and also studied as models for further construction. St Nicholas's is clearly based on a Romanesque design. With its great chancel arch and narrow doorways, and with three of the original windows still in the nave, the church speaks well for the standards imposed by the king. It served, as did so many churches then, as a refuge against Danish attackers, and still looks solid and more sure of itself than the once vast forest beside whose remains it stands.

Christianity had been virtually driven out of England by its heathen conquerors. It had at best been the religion of the more cultured, Romanised Britons, and when they were scattered their beliefs and rituals were blown away with them. Only the priests and monks of the Celtic church, working in isolation from the church of Rome, continued to preach in the westernmost parts of the land, gradually probing back into the regions of which they had been dispossessed. They converted a minor king here, courageously planted a monastery there. When the Pope sent Augustine to preach the word of God to the English nation, and these Angles and Saxons began to abandon their Germanic gods, there was some dispute as to whether the Celtic calendar and usages were compatible with those of Rome.

Procedural and sectarian differences were thrashed out at the Synod of Whitby in A.D. 664 where Wilfrid, Bishop of York, was one of the strongest advocates of Roman doctrines.

Earlier that same year Wilfrid had paid an unpremeditated visit to Sussex. The ship in which he was returning from his consecration as bishop in Compiègne went aground in a storm, and he and his companions were attacked by local scoundrels eager for plunder. Fortunately the tide floated the vessel away before its occupants could be overpowered, and Wilfrid went off to assume responsibility for his diocese.

He found it a troublesome burden, and after disputes with the Northumbrian king was driven out. After travelling in England and abroad, he came back at last to the land of the South Saxons where he had been so rudely treated years ago. Although the region was still predominantly pagan, its king had been converted to Christianity, and a Scottish or Irish monk named Dicul was allowed to share a small monastery at Bosham with a handful of devout companions: even though, as Bede lamented, 'none of the natives was willing to follow their way of life or listen to their teaching'.

Granted land by the king near Selsey, Wilfrid plunged into the work of salvation. He baptised the leading men of the province and their wives, and also offered more mundane guidance. Afflicted by a protracted drought and, in spite of the length of their peninsular coast, knowing nothing about fishing, the people were dying of starvation and sometimes drowning themselves in groups of 40 or more rather than suffer the pangs of hunger any further. From the moment St Wilfrid began to preach, a soft rainfall restored green to the fields; and while the joyful converts awaited the new crops, he taught them how to fish. He founded a monastery, a cathedral, and an episcopal palace on his 'Seals' Island' – all of it now somewhere beneath the sea off present-day Selsey.

It took the threat of another wave of pagan invaders to persuade the now Christianised Saxons to build more substantially for this life as well as the next. The individualistic lords, warriors and farmers must stand more closely together if they were to survive. The devastations of the Danes were halted only when Alfred set up his garrisons in a chain of 'burhs' or fortified places. One of these made use of the remaining Roman defences of Chichester, from which in A.D. 895 a particularly savage raid was thrown back in disorder by the townsmen, who also laid their hands on several of the Danish longships.

The impact of the Danes on Sussex was less than that on most other parts of the country. Once the few Roman roads to the east, west and north-east had been abandoned, the Weald and all that lay south of it was again cut off from most outside influences. This was one reason why paganism had lingered here when much of the rest of England had been converted. Military occupation and gentler conquests had all to begin and be consummated along the narrow littoral. It all took ships and supplies. The Danes might make occasional raids, but on the whole found it more rewarding to concentrate on the nearer, east coasts. The next major assault, however, struck Sussex first, and struck it most grievously.

King Edward the Confessor had been brought up in Normandy during the time when Canute, the Dane, reigned over England. When he returned he found that he had few things in common with the arrogant Saxon nobles who had engineered his accession to the throne. He married the daughter of the most powerful of them, Earl Godwin of Wessex; then quarrelled with Godwin over an insult offered on the earl's land to one of his Norman friends; but had to climb down in the face of threats from Godwin and

Harold, son of Godwin. After the earl's death, Harold became the most powerful man in Wessex and in the royal councils. Distressed by the brutalities of power politics, the Confessor allowed himself to become more and more absorbed in religious observances and in the building of a mighty abbey at Westminster.

In 1064 Harold set sail from Bosham, where his family had extensive property, on a voyage whose purpose remains shrouded in mystery to this day. It has been suggested that he was off on a pleasure cruise; but he is shown on the Bayeux Tapestry about to attend mass in Bosham church, implying that something serious lay ahead. Another theory is that he was travelling to Normandy to bring home a younger brother from the banishment earlier imposed by King Edward. Whatever his intentions, and whether by design or as a result of an unfavourable wind, he reached the French coast and was promptly taken prisoner and handed over to Duke William of Normandy.

The rest of the story appears in innumerable history books in varying forms, according to the sympathies of the author. Harold was either tricked into promising William support in the Norman's claim to the throne of England when the Confessor died, or he gave the promise voluntarily and then treacherously changed his mind. Treachery or no treachery, he certainly allowed himself to be proclaimed king by the council of the Witan after Edward's death.

He and his supporters knew that William would be enraged and must soon be expected on their doorstep. Fighting men were assembled, but while they were preparing for a Norman attack on the south coast news came of a Norwegian invasion in the north-east. Harold had to take his troops by forced marches to Stamford Bridge, where they defeated the Norsemen. Almost before he could draw breath, messengers arrived to report that the Normans had landed on the Sussex coast.

6   *Lancing College Chapel*

Duke William had been expecting fierce opposition when he set foot on shore, traditionally near Pevensey, though some associate the landing with Bulverhythe, between Bexhill and Hastings. But there was no one to hinder the disembarkation. The only mishap was William's own first step, which sent him sprawling on the beach. He turned it to good advantage, brandishing a handful of sand and shouting, 'By the grace of God I have taken hold of my kingdom.'

Learning where Harold had gone, and determined to be firmly entrenched before his return, William marched on Hastings, ravaging the land and cowing any flicker of potential resistance as he went. He set the townsfolk to strengthening the wooden fortifications of the castle, on the same hill as the present ruins of his own later, more substantial building.

Harold's battle-weary forces took six days to reach London. Instead of waiting there for reinforcements he ordered ships out of the Thames to take the Normans in the rear, while he and his foot soldiers marched along trackways through the eastern stretches of the Weald. They reached Caldbec Hill, a few miles north-west of Hastings, to find William on the move, having decided either to risk a march on London or to find a strategic point at which to confront the Saxons.

The Saxons in fact had the superior position. Harold came forward from Caldbec to the slightly lower ridge of Senlac, and arrayed his men along it on a half-mile front. For the Normans it would be literally an uphill fight all the way.

On the morning of 14 October 1066 began what was to be the last successful battle fought on British soil by the invasion forces of a foreign power.

In numbers the two sides were fairly evenly matched. In makeup they differed considerably. William had brought

7-10 *Churches at: (above left) Sompting; (above right) Southease; (bottom left) Steyning; (bottom right) Berwick*

with him 3,500 horses for his armoured knights, fearsome once they had gathered momentum but severely hampered when confronted by a steep slope and the impenetrable shield wall of the Saxons. For Harold's part, he had no fighting cavalry, but was confident that all would be well if that shield wall could hold firm and let each onslaught of horsemen or infantry break against it, while his house-carls, the professional nucleus of an otherwise part-time army called in from the fields and hamlets, wrought havoc with their double-handed axes.

Quite early in the day one flank of the invading army collapsed in panic. It consisted mainly of Breton adventurers and mercenaries who had come with William in search of easy loot, and found it was not going to come all that easily. As they fled, some of Harold's shire levies disobeyed orders and pursued them downhill, whereupon the mounted knights showed how efficient they could be when given an opportunity. The same thing happened again, round about noon. William's admirers were later to record this as a brilliant tactical manoeuvre, luring more of the Saxons down on to the level and there annihilating them. Others attribute it to a panic as real as the first one. In any case, the battle was still not settled but continued until about an hour before sunset. Late in the day the Normans stopped wasting their arrows against Saxon shields and fired them upwards in deadly parabolas; and continuous assaults against the shield wall began at last to breach it.

Harold himself was killed in the closing hours of the struggle. The legend that his death resulted from an arrow through the eye probably derives from a misinterpretation of part of the Bayeux Tapestry. What appears more likely is that he was struck down beside his standard and then dispatched by the sword of a Norman knight. When his corpse was later recovered from the carnage, William decreed that it should have no other grave than a stone cairn on the shore, but later allowed its burial in the abbey which Harold had founded at Waltham in Essex.

William the Conqueror in his turn founded an abbey, as he had sworn to do if granted victory. He had also promised William Faber, a monk in his service, that the foundation should be dedicated to St Martin, and when reminded of this pledge he appointed Faber to supervise building work on the hilltop where the Normans had triumphed. In their monarch's absence, Faber and his brethren decided that the battlefield was in an uncomfortably exposed position and would be difficult to supply with water; so they started work farther down the slope. When William heard of this he went into one of the rages for which he was noted. The monastery was hurriedly recommenced on the summit, with its church's high altar on the spot where Harold had been killed.

In the late twelfth century the then abbot adorned the church and built a marble cloister, and in the following century there was lavish rebuilding and the addition of a guest-house. In 1338 it was all fortified, and it was at this time that the mighty gatehouse which still dominates the centre of Battle was built. At the Dissolution of the Monasteries, Henry VIII gave the house and all that went with it to Sir Anthony Browne, his master of horse. After Henry's death Browne became Princess Elizabeth's guardian, and among other secular additions to his property conceived the idea of a worthy lodging for his royal charge. An extensive house was constructed, but most of it was pulled down in the eighteenth and nineteenth centuries, leaving only two spindly watch-towers. The remaining buildings form, today, a girls' school.

Sir Anthony's pride in his historic possessions may have been somewhat disturbed by a curse laid upon him by one of the monks ejected from the abbey. His line, it was declared, should perish by fire and water. This was grimly fulfilled: in 1793 Browne's direct descendant, the eighth Viscount Montague, was drowned while holidaying on the Rhine, just as a message was on its way to inform him that his home, Cowdray Castle in West Sussex, had been burned down. The estate passed to his sister . . . and both her sons were drowned. Although the line was undoubtedly thus destroyed, there are those who believe that the curse still retains some aimlessly malevolent power: how else explain the fire which in 1931 gutted the abbot's house, remodelled for his own use by Sir Anthony?

To the best of my knowledge there are no stories of any curse imposed on the district by the defeated Saxons, or of any reproachful ghosts walking the streets and hillside. I have, however, found myself shivering uncontrollably, even in bright sunshine, when passing one steep cleft below the battlefield – perhaps the ditch, running red with blood, in which took place the final slaughter, or, as we so clinically put it nowadays, the 'mopping-up operations'.

William was quite ruthless in the pacification of his new country. He distributed the estates of Saxon landowners lavishly among his followers, exacted a brutal revenge on anyone known to have opposed him, and burned and slaughtered his way across the rebellious north of England.

Twenty years after his victory at Battle, the Conqueror decided to draw up a list of his assets, comparing the population and possessions of every estate with those at the time of his accession. After a first intensive survey there was a second, carried out by men not known in the areas they were assessing, 'in order that they might have an opportunity to check the first survey and, if necessary, denounce its authors as guilty to the king'. So implacable was this inquisition that men spoke of the Day of Judgment, and of the final collection of documents as Domesday Book.

From the figures given in the survey it is possible to

estimate the total population of the country at the time as a million and a quarter, with slightly more than 50,000 in Sussex. By the beginning of the nineteenth century the county had nearly 160,000 inhabitants; then there was a striking upsurge throughout the century, until at its end the figure was 605,000. In our present century so far it has just about doubled.

Many entries stress the importance of fish and the salting down of fish to the economy of the region. The lord of the manor of Bristelmestune (Brighton) received a rent in kind from his tenants amounting to some 4,000 herring, and other similar rents were frequently paid in salted fish. Salt extracted from evaporating pans along the coast and in the estuaries, each duly valued and charged by William's tax inspectors, was used for preserving meat, but especially for preserving fish for use in Lent and on other fast days.

*   *   *

The Norman administrative divisions split the county, as we noted earlier, into six, referred to in Domesday Book and thereafter as Rapes. From west to east there were: Chichester and Arundel (at the outset combined under one powerful baron); Bramber; Lewes; Pevensey; and Hastings. Although based logically enough on the main rivers and accompanying ports, backed by large inland castles and smaller motte and bailey castles under the control of William's most trusted lords, they have little significance for the modern traveller, who can cross their boundary lines without noticing any marked change in the landscape. He can scarcely travel south to north without realising the distinction between the coastal strip, the Downs, the Weald and the northern ridge.

In this book I have chosen to travel west to east along the coast, with an occasional foray up the river valleys, then turned back along the Downs, and finally plunged into the western Weald and explored it to its eastern extremity. To me it makes sense; but anyone who turns off to pursue a tempting by-way, or defiantly trespass on one of the parallel swathes of hill or lowland, will undoubtedly find equally satisfactory routes – I have done so many a time – and is entitled to declare any such choice superior.

In Sussex it is still almost impossible to take a chance and not be richly rewarded.

CHAPTER TWO

Chichester Harbour to Brighton

The Manhood region, which has witnessed so many invasions large and small, now sees an even busier traffic on its waters. Every inlet of the little River Lavant's convoluted estuary has its moorings, its sailing club, its smartly converted cottages and its pubs resonant with that hearty booming which characterises the owner of even the most diminutive sailing dinghy, as though it were constantly necessary to make oneself heard across a wide harbour in a howling gale. Even in the heart of the peninsula, with great fields resembling those of the Fens, though much less sombre, and with great greenhouses dazzling under the sun, the pubs have nautical names. Sidlesham, for example, a straggling village equally remote in spirit from the holiday-camp world of near-by Bognor and from the thickets of masts in the yacht basins, has its *Anchor* and *Jolly Fisherman*. But then, the vagaries of the coastline here have turned many an anchorage into a rural hamlet, many a fertile pasture into mud on the sea bed.

Approaching this coast, we are in a world of salt flats intersected by innumerable little streams known locally as rifes; a world of geese and waders; and then, abruptly, of caravan sites, chalets, holiday villages and rubbish-littered sands. East Wittering is all bungalows and cafés. West Wittering, trying to maintain a tone of slightly arch respectability, is nevertheless turning into an equally popular resort. Yet the air is so sparkling, and the views to the east and across to the Isle of Wight so exhilarating, that it would be unreasonable to begrudge people their enjoyment of holidays here.

47

Dell Quay, sheltered in an arm of the haven, is all boats and an admirable inn. The surrounding district of Appledram was once a centre of salt production – and salt smuggling. Its most impressive feature is the fine fifteenth-century stone house of Rymans, whose gardens are sometimes open to the public. There is a story that its original owner decided to fortify his manor and to this end imported large quantities of Caen stone. The king, however, was suspicious of subjects who wished to turn their homes into castles, and forbade him to proceed, upon which the stone was given to Chichester Cathedral, where it is to be found in the bell tower.

At near-by Birdham, Turner conceived the magnificent painting of the harbour which hangs in Petworth House. The sixteenth-century church here has a low door through which it is said the devil was kicked out, after which the door was hastily sealed up to make sure he didn't scurry back in again.

The name of the Manhood derives from a word meaning 'the common wood', in this case the wood where the regional Hundred assembled for its regular discussions. William of Malmesbury tells how Alfred the Great 'appointed centuries, which they call "hundreds", and decennaries, that is to say "tithings".' Each Hundred covered an area containing 100 heads of households, who were made responsible for maintenance of law and order and for rallying to their king in time of war. The ecclesiastical division known as the parish also dates from this Anglo–Saxon era.

Local place names testify eloquently to Saxon influence. Obliteration of the Celts had been so complete that, even where groups or individuals were suffered to stay, most likely as slaves, no trace of their language remained in common usage. The only unarguably identifiable Celtic names lingering in Sussex are those of two rivers, the Lavant and the Tarrant, this latter being the old name for the Arun. Saxon settlements are clearly defined in a certain sequence. Where we find large numbers of names ending in 'ham', such as Pagham, Bosham, and so many others in the Manhood region, it is pretty certain to be a region settled early in the Saxon era. The word signifies a farm or homestead. Cakeham, between the Witterings, is Cacca's home, Bracklesham Braccol's home. The suffix is to be found right across the county from Barnham to Ashburnham, and in forms such as Bodiam and Northiam. Occasionally there are possible confusions with the ending 'hamm', often contracted to 'ham', which can mean water meadows: thus the little River Tillingham near Rye is likelier to be the water meadow of Tilli's people than their homestead.

Later settlements are distinguished by 'tun' or 'ton', meaning an enclosure and hence in due course a village or town. Examples are Middleton, Plumpton, and one which has gone through many transmogrifications from Bristelmestune to Brighton.

Another early appearance was the 'ingas' ending. Added to a proper name, 'ing' identified a son or other descendant, while 'ingas' meant a whole lineage or followers of a certain chieftain. Angmering was the place of the people of Angenmaer, Wittering of Withhere's followers; and Hastings, as we have noted, that of the followers of Haesten.

Bosham, set picturesquely on a wide creek to the west of Chichester and Fishbourne, is today a haunt of writers, painters and yachtsmen. When the tide is out, cars are parked along the road and green-slimed pebbles below high tide line; when it is in, incongruous traffic signs jut up from the water like half-submerged groyne markers, and in the shallows one can make out the white blobs of 'give way' paint – more appropriate for paddlers or motor boats than for motor cars. Unlike many places of such charm and such an enviable setting, the village has not lost its identity. Small as its nucleus is, it remains imposing, even imperious. It has seen almost too much history : prehistoric immigrants, the Belgae, Vespasian, Saxons and Danes; and is unshakeable in its claim to being the oldest site of Christianity in Sussex.

The cell in which Dicul and his fellow monks prayed in pagan times is thought to be under the crypt of the present church. The Saxon tower has been adapted from what was once a watch-tower commanding all the waterways along which Danish marauders might infiltrate. The legend is recounted of one such crew which succeeded in making away with the tenor bell from the monastery, only to have it drown them in the creek by breaking through the bottom of their ship. It settled into what became known as the Bell Hole and has ever since, to some psychically sensitive ears, added an answering harmony to the peal from the church belfry.

It was a Dane to whom we owe much of the existing church. King Canute was probably responsible for converting the tower and building the nave, and another of the old traditions is that of his daughter's burial within the church. Sceptics have denied this; but in 1865 the then incumbent instructed masons engaged in repair work to examine the spot beneath which the child was supposed to lie. They found a small stone coffin containing the remains of a child of about eight, which fitted the story. The coffin, together with one containing bones of an impressively proportioned man, was exposed again in 1954 when the present floor was laid, and there is now a memorial plaque in Royal Copenhagen porcelain bearing Canute's emblem, the black raven.

The most famous tale about Canute is also associated with Bosham. Forty years ago the National Trust was presented with the acre of Quay Meadow between church and creek, this being the supposed stretch of land from which the king ordered the sea to recede. Southampton claims the honour in its own Canute Road; but you would be ill advised to argue the matter in Bosham.

This meadow is also, more authentically, the spot from which Harold set out on his ill-fated voyage in 1064. Earl Godwin had a manor at Bosham, and in fact owned all the land between Chichester and Havant, which on his death passed to his son Harold. After Harold's own death at Senlac, William seized the estates for himself and in due course presented the manor to the first bishop of the see of Chichester, created in place of that of Selsey.

Selsey Bill, on the tip of this eventful peninsula, is also the southernmost tip of Sussex. Somewhere off its hard sands, ideal today for riding, may lie St Wilfrid's old monastery and cathedral. To the west are the remarkable fossil beds of Bracklesham.

Selsey parish church is an oddity, having been split in two so that its separate sections stand about a mile and a half apart. The original building, developed between the twelfth and fifteenth centuries around a priory associated with St Wilfrid, stood at Church Norton above Pagham Harbour. When Selsey began to grow, it did so in a southerly direction, leaving its parish church of St Peter some distance behind it. In the middle of the nineteenth century it was decided to bring the church to the congregation rather than expect the congregation to trek out of town to the church. Bodily transference of the building was not impracticable, but ecclesiastical law would not permit the removal of the chancel. Piece by piece, therefore, the fabric, the Purbeck and Sussex marble font, the old processional porch, pillars and oak roof were carried in farm wagons to a new site, leaving the truncated chancel where it was. The west end was sealed, and in 1917 the lonely little building was re-named St Wilfrid's Chapel.

Surrounded by a graveyard, the chapel is now used

largely for funerals. Its east window was presented in memory of the donor's wife and of his brother and a friend killed in the First World War. The almost photographic sepia likenesses of the three people enhaloed in the stained glass produces a disturbingly anachronistic effect.

The approach to the chapel is delightful: a lane through an avenue of trees, showering in autumn a bronze confetti, leads to a small arc of woodland sheltering the graveyard . . . and then, opening up beyond, is a great expanse of saltings, mud and unstable shingle.

This is Pagham Harbour, now a nature reserve of tidal marshland, where wildfowl and waders spend the winter, and the little tern breeds. There are bristly, crumpled stretches of breakwater and ragged stumps, relics of many a vain attempt to keep the harbour clear. A helpful notice-board identifies the paths open to the public. It is a place for those who like to be alone, and to be still – if one can call it stillness when there is always a breeze, always the whisper of water and grasses and the flurry of birds.

Almost a century ago a writer could say of Middleton and Pagham that they matched each other 'in the absence of all picturesque beauty and an equally active agency of destruction'. Destruction always threatened: silting-up in one place, inundation in another. In returns submitted on the taxable and rateable values of their lands, many parishes had good reason to complain that the value had diminished because the land itself was diminishing. Today Middleton is an eastern extension of Bognor; and to the west Bognor is crowding in on Pagham, too.

With its choked harbour, Pagham ceased to be a major port. Nor does it any longer have a palace for visiting archbishops of Canterbury, though they remain patrons of the benefice. Its church is dedicated to one of the greatest of them, St Thomas à Becket, who came frequently to

Pagham. One of his many disputes with Henry II arose from questions concerning a manor under his lordship here, and his trusted secretary and biographer, Herbert of Bosham, was a local man and is believed to have been buried at Bosham.

At the beginning of the last century Pagham church was in poor shape, and after a severe storm had to be declared unfit for use. It was then restored, some parts being completely rebuilt. The modern glass was presented by Sir Arthur du Cros as a thank-offering for the recovery of King George V, who, after a serious illness, spent part of his convalescence in 1929 at Sir Arthur's near-by home.

In spite of Canterbury's interests in the region, the Selsey peninsula ceased to be of great ecclesiastical significance after the Norman Conquest. William I decided to transfer episcopal power from St Wilfrid's old see to a new one in Chichester, and work began there on a great cathedral.

Chichester had dwindled in importance since Roman times, but now began its climb to a new eminence. The builders of the new edifice appear to have followed some of King Alfred's precepts, choosing a site which must once have been highly regarded by the Romans and utilising what was left of their handiwork as a basis for fresh construction: widespread indications of these earlier buildings and a number of mosaic pavements have come to light during recent repairs and examinations.

Six years after the cathedral's consecration there was a serious fire, which proved to be the first of several over the years; but much twelfth- and thirteenth-century work survives. Early in the eighteenth century the spire was struck by lightning, which, according to Daniel Defoe, 'drove several great stones out of the steeple, and carried them clear off, not from the roof of the church only, but of the adjacent houses also, and they were found at a prodigious distance from the steeple, so that they must have been shot out of a cannon, or blown out of a mine'. In 1861 the whole spire collapsed, but five years later was restored in the same style under the supervision of Sir Gilbert Scott. The bells are housed in a separate campanile, one of the few detached bell towers in the country.

One of the most recent additions to the cathedral is John Piper's flamboyant tapestry behind the altar. Although the somewhat sombre interior can undoubtedly profit from such a clash of colour, I was tempted at first sight to call it garish. But a regular communicant assures me that there is a world of difference between the tapestry seen 'cold' as one walks through the cathedral analysing this, that and the other, and the tapestry seen during a service, when it comes to life and illumines the whole place. The artist could hardly ask for a worthier tribute.

By the cloisters runs the walled St Richard's Walk, commemorating a well-loved bishop whose tomb became a place of pilgrimage even before his canonisation. Ordained by the Bishop of Orléans in 1243, Richard found it difficult to take up duties in his diocese, since King Henry III had already forced the canons of Chichester to appoint a lackey of his own, and refused to acknowledge their change of heart when they dared to elect Richard in his place. Appealed to by Richard, the Pope confirmed his appointment, whereupon the king seized all the diocese's estates and revenue. When Richard tried to enter the city, armed with the Pope's mandate, he learned that Henry had expressly forbidden anyone to shelter him or provide him with funds.

In spite of this royal decree, Richard was sheltered by a humble monk in the village of Ferring, from where he went out preaching and offering what spiritual succour he could to the peasants within his see. He ceaselessly demanded the return of all that the king had seized, and when the Pope finally threatened excommunication Henry surrendered. Richard was insistent on all the rights and splendours due to his office, but years as a mendicant friar had blunted any personal appetite for luxury, and his concern remained always for the poor. Many miracles in the feeding of the needy are attributed to him while still alive, and after his death many more in the healing of sickness at his shrine in the cathedral, before the altar of St Edmund. He had especially venerated this saint, and died just after consecrating a church to him in Dover.

To Simon, the priest of Ferring who had given him shelter and spiritual support, he bequeathed his favourite horse and a commentary on the Psalms.

Defoe in his time observed of Chichester that 'if six or seven good families were removed, there would not be much conversation, except what is to be found among the canons, and dignitaries of the cathedral'. It is the sort of criticism all too easy to make about the older cathedral cities, and often all too justifiable. It is hardly true of Chichester today. There seem always to be lively arguments going on there – about the by-pass, the theatre, the traffic, or possibilities at Goodwood. Some lively publishing houses have their home here, and in one admirable bookshop you can drink coffee and wrangle all day to your heart's content.

The four Roman roads form an excellent shopping centre – or, rather, form four excellent spokes from the central market cross. If the traffic does tend to snarl up around this hub, it will do the drivers no harm to control their impatience and study the stonework. Better that than clumsily knocking chunks off it. The cross, dating from 1501, no longer shelters merchants and farmers bringing their produce into town; anyone who does risk seeking a refuge under its beautiful arches is likely to be marooned for quite some time while waiting for a gap in the swirl of cars; but it is still the lovely pivot of the city, and its clock, however late an addition to the original structure, has become an integral part of it.

There are no prescribed itineraries for the visitor. You may choose to make a general reconnaissance from the Georgian promenades along stretches of the old walls, on their Roman and medieval foundations, or strike off directly into the Georgian streets themselves. Most rewarding are the four known as the Pallants, each house in which is listed as of special historic or architectural value. The name derives from the palatine jurisdiction once exercised by the archbishops of Canterbury. Inevitably their noble doorways are accompanied by the brass plates of solicitors, accountants and tax collectors who seem to breathe most happily in cathedral precincts or their immediate proximity.

In Priory Park is the surviving chancel of a thirteenth-century Franciscan priory church, now a museum of church history and of archaeological discoveries in the district. And in Oaklands Park is the building by which modern Chichester is perhaps best known throughout the country.

In South Street there was once a theatre, converted in the middle of the eighteenth century from a malthouse. By 1850 it was slipping back into its old ways, having been turned into a brewhouse. Later it became a Mechanics' Reading Room, a gymnasium, a branch of the county library, a furniture repository and, in our own day, an antique market. In his monograph on the theatre's history we find Francis Steer in 1957 hoping that it 'will one day be restored and the intentions of its builders will be continued after an interval of more than a century'. His wish was not granted. Instead, something more remarkable happened.

One evening in January 1959 Leslie Evershed-Martin, who had served many years on the city council and twice been mayor, was watching a television programme dealing with the adventurous Shakespeare Theatre in Stratford, Ontario. Tyrone Guthrie's account of how this Canadian theatre

11 *Royal Crescent, Brighton*

came into being as a community effort, and how successful its architectural and dramatic experiments had proved, fired Mr Evershed-Martin's imagination. He decided that Chichester was the ideal place for an equally daring venture and, with the support of his family and a growing number of loyal friends, overcame early scepticism and a whole complex of financial and administrative problems. All the money was to be raised from voluntary subscribers: not a penny, he was resolved, should be asked for from the rates. The auditorium must not be the conventional type, but should be built around a thrust stage, so that instead of staring at the intrinsically two-dimensional patterns of the orthodox proscenium stage the audience would almost surround and be involved in the action.

In May 1961 the foundation stone was laid in Oaklands Park by Princess Alexandra, and on 5 July 1962 the Chichester Festival Theatre opened its doors for its first performance. Some critics were unhappy with the open stage. Some felt that the production of John Fletcher's *The Chances* was not the happiest choice to launch such an ambitious project. But the carpers were gradually muted. Sir Laurence Olivier, the theatre's first director, set his seal upon the place when directing and appearing in *Uncle Vanya*, and when he became director of the National Theatre used its resources for the next three Chichester Festival seasons. In 1966 John Clements took over and, as Lord Olivier generously acknowledges, 'has more than doubled the interest in the place'.

Well may Leslie Evershed-Martin quote *Coriolanus:*

> *I have lived*
> *To see inherited my very wishes*
> *And the buildings of my fancy.*

Any road out of Chichester leads to a number of delights, but if we head west we are liable to run off the edge of

12 *Royal Pavilion, Brighton*

Sussex into Hampshire. Let us instead try a few miles of Roman road to the north-east.

*   *   *

Stane Street begins at the end of St Pancras Road and, as the A.285, climbs beyond Halnaker towards the Downs. Halnaker Hill still has the windmill, refurbished by the county council in 1972, which Hilaire Belloc admired almost as much as his own at Shipley. Below are the remains of Halnaker House, for a time the home of the De La Warrs, and down a side road is an architectural gem which they saved from demolition.

Boxgrove Priory was founded by Benedictines in 1105. At the time of the Dissolution, Lord De la Warr was engaged in building a chantry in which he intended eventually to be buried. Rather than see it destroyed, he pleaded to buy the priory back from the Crown, and was allowed to do so; though in the end he was laid to rest not here but at Broadwater, above Worthing. Thanks to his gesture, much of the original Norman fabric survives. The nave and the north and south transepts are unspoilt, and later work represents some of the finest features of differing periods: the thirteenth-century vaulting is the only remaining example of its kind in the country, the chantry itself is a superb piece of Renaissance craftsmanship, and there is a fine painted ceiling of about the same age above the choir.

Since in visiting Boxgrove we have turned away from the hills, we may as well continue towards the coast, obeying all the road signs pointing to the holiday magnet of the region, Bognor.

The route takes us past Tangmere, the airfield which, during the Battle of Britain and onwards throughout the Second World War, contributed so much to ensuring that the Nazis were unable to follow in the footsteps of Romans,

Saxons and Normans along these shores. Its village church is a mixture of Norman and Early English, with a thirteenth-century timbered bell turret. These timbered bell-cotes occur in a number of attractive forms all over the county. There are many tall, shingled spires, and many more squat, simple pyramids, known as the 'Sussex cap'.

The village from which Bognor developed was Bersted, a mile inland. It remained insignificant until the late eighteenth century, when a rich hatter and M.P., Sir Richard Hotham, planned to make it a rival to Brighton and endeavoured, without success, to have it renamed Hothampton. A hotel and assembly rooms were laid out; the building of select residences carefully supervised – 'only carriage owners encouraged', as Pevsner puts it. Princess Charlotte, one of George III's daughters, was tempted into paying the town a visit. Princess Victoria, later to become queen, stayed with her mother for some time at Bognor Lodge, originally built by Sir Richard for himself. In the twentieth century came the ultimate royal accolade when George V, having grown fond of the town during his convalescence, decreed that it should be known in future as Bognor Regis.

Its Georgian backbone saves it from collapse. In spite of the amusement arcades, the esplanade, the pier and the holiday camp, it retains a wistful shabby-genteel air, and behind the frayed façade protects its prouder memories. It would take really determined Philistines to spoil Waterloo Square – though there is regrettably no lack of such folk about – and in spite of its boating lake and little train and its attraction for holidaymakers, Hotham Park remains primarily the preserve of local residents: young mothers with their prams or with toddlers in the playground, and old ladies gossiping amiably without taking their eyes off the passers-by. Hotham House, around which the park was built, has long been in danger of condemnation and demolition, but sturdy efforts continue to be made for its preservation.

However select or selective it wished to be at the start, Bognor has emulated other seaside resorts in its greedy absorption of neighbouring villages and hamlets. Among them was Felpham, where, in a thatched cottage which still happily exists, William Blake lived for three years. He called it 'the sweetest spot on earth', even went so far as to declare 'Heaven is there', and was privileged to witness a fairy's funeral. The road past his cottage is now known as Blake's Lane.

The poet came here as a result of his friendship with the philanthropic William Hayley, whose *Life of Cowper* was enriched by Blake's engravings. Hayley had previously lived at Eartham, on a slope of the Downs a few miles to the north, but sold his home there after the death of his wife and son, and moved to Felpham. He is buried in the parish church.

The next owner of the house at Eartham suffered a historic misfortune. He was William Huskisson, M.P. for Chichester, who was the first man to be killed by a railway train, when struck by Stephenson's *Rocket* at the opening of the Liverpool and Manchester Railway. There is a statue to him in Chichester Cathedral, and a memorial in Eartham church.

Felpham runs on now into Middleton, and once we are clear of that we are already close to the golf links and so to Littlehampton at the mouth of the Arun.

This is the first of the river divisions adopted by the Normans, with an important harbour at the mouth and a guardian castle higher upstream. It was the main port of entry for Caen stone and other shipments from Normandy, and was also used for more eventful landings: immediately after the death of William the Conqueror, his son William Rufus hurried in through this port to make sure that he, rather than his older brother, would be proclaimed king; and Matilda arrived in similar haste to claim the throne in 1125.

Today the harbour is the preserve mainly of yachtsmen and power-boat enthusiasts. I still recall with gratitude one establishment not far from the water's edge. Towards the end of a hot day when I had driven from half-way across the county with a hungry family, the words 'fish and chips' were rashly uttered. There is something spellbinding about the mere mention of this commodity, something which has nothing in common with the desire for a nice piece of steak, a glass of wine or a pint of ale. Once one has allowed oneself to think of fish and ships, the craving cannot be assuaged by any substitute. But on this day we drove on and on, with two small boys growing more and more desperate: everywhere closed, not a sight of a crumpled newspaper and the characteristic dabbing motion of a hand into it, not a waft of that unmistakable aroma. Then in Littlehampton we found a shop open, serving what seemed then and in retrospect still seems the best fish and chips I have ever tasted.

There was a time when Arundel, up-river, was a port of some consequence in itself, as well as providing a sentinel castle to watch over the Arun's gap in the Downs. By the middle of the sixteenth century a profitable timber trade had been established along its busy wharves, and there was a small but vigorous ship-building industry. Strenuous efforts had continually to be made to keep the tideway clear and check silting-up around Littlehampton.

The river, as we noted earlier, was originally the Tarrant. Its present name derives from the town, rather than the other way round. Arundel is not, as might appear, the dell or dale of the Arun, but the dale of the hoarhound, from the Old English *harhundell*. It should be mentioned, though, that some have claimed to recognise in it one of the rare

Celtic survivals, meaning 'the high place on the water meadows'.

The approach by water through these meadows, even if now we can make it only by canoe or rowing-boat, is still the finest. The castle rises shimmering and resplendent from its spur on the Downs, with a rich back-drop of trees, and even the knowledge that most of its convincingly medieval features are late nineteenth-century fantasies cannot detract from the effect.

Before the Conquest the castle may have been only a simple drystone structure, strengthened by Alfred the Great and then allowed to decline until only a massive keep remained on a high artificial mound. When William I dealt out favours to knights who had stood beside him at the battle of Hastings and helped subdue later rebellions, he created the 'Honour of Arundel', covering the Rapes of both Chichester and Arundel, and made Roger de Montgomery its earl. Montgomery thus owned more than 80 manors, which he leased to lesser knights in return for their military loyalty and financial assistance. He used imported Caen stone and local Pulborough stone to extend the castle, adding such features as the great gatehouse and Bevis tower, so called after a giant Bevis who is said to have been warder of the castle.

Roger's son Robert grew arrogant like so many of his fellow barons and rebelled against Henry I, as a result of which his stronghold was confiscated. It passed through various hands until 1580, when by marriage it came into the possession of Thomas Howard, Earl of Surrey and third Duke of Norfolk. Apart from some troubles in Elizabeth's reign it has remained in the family ever since. It was to the fifteenth Duke of Norfolk that we owe the restoration at the end of the last century, as well as the Roman Catholic cathedral of St Philip Neri. The eastern end of the parish church of St Nicholas is also Roman Catholic, divided by a wall from the Anglican congregation in the west.

The castle was besieged at two other points in history. The first was when Matilda appeared in England and was accorded reluctant hospitality here, which brought Stephen hurrying to lay siege before she could rally supporters against his claim to kingship. Somehow he was persuaded to withdraw without inflicting any damage. Real disaster befell only during the Civil War.

At the outset Parliament knew that control of the Channel ports and the Wealden iron industry was essential. In general the Sussex gentry favoured the Parliamentary cause, and although the personal loyalties or personal fears of many of the poorer classes might lead them to support a local lord in the cause of King Charles, there was little stomach for a bitter fight. In a matter of months most of the Royalists had been brought into line: Arundel fell without a struggle, Chichester was besieged for six days and then surrendered, and Cavaliers trying to reach Lewes were defeated at Haywards Heath.

In late 1643 Arundel was taken unawares by a Royalist force under Lord Hopton, profiting from an unusually severe frost which hardened the usually impassable mire of winter. Before the weather could break, Sir William Waller marched his men from Farnham to Arundel and subjected the castle to a vengeful bombardment. Some of the worst damage was done by cannon firing down into the defenders from the tower of St Nicholas's church. The church itself was used as a barracks, despoiled, and had all its stained glass windows shattered.

On 6 January 1644 the garrison surrendered, and the whole county remained effectively under Parliamentary control for the rest of the war.

Associated with this last siege and bombardment is the sad story of young William Springet and his wife. A staunch young Puritan of good family, Springet raised a regiment of horse at the beginning of the war. After the capture of Arundel, he and Colonel Morley were given charge of the castle; but Springet soon fell ill with a fever known as calenture, more familiar to sailors of the time than to landsmen, characterised by a delirium in which the sufferer fancied the sea to be green fields and longed to throw himself into it. His wife was in London in an advanced state of pregnancy, but when the news reached her she set off at once for Arundel. The notoriously bad roads of the county were flooded and she had difficulty engaging a coach. Standard rates for transport hire were established at about this time but specifically exempted 'Sussex roads, which being worst and hardest for journeying shall be travelled as far only as is reasonable or shall be agreed or undertaken by the coachman upon hire'. After fixing the price – a high one – and setting out, the young wife found that in some places they had virtually 'to row in the highways in a boat . . . and to swim the coach and horses in the highways'.

Longing to reach Arundel, she was nevertheless appalled when at last it came in view. Buildings and windows were smashed, and soldiers were turning all available accommodation into stables. She came to her husband's side late at night, and sat with him for two days. He died, being only 23, and his own ammunition wagon carried the body to his own village of Ringmer.

Later his widow remarried and became a Quaker. She also became the mother-in-law of the William Penn who was to give his name to Pennsylvania.

Below Arundel Park, on a curve of the river, is the *Black Rabbit*, which has been an inn since 1793. The town huddled below the castle still looks feudal, not to say obsequious; yet local folk have not been chary of challenging their lord when it has suited them. In the middle of the last century the duke decided to close the way into the park past the

Black Rabbit. This incensed those who had always regarded it as a public right of way, and there must have been some rowdy discussions and a great deal of banging of pots on the bar within the hostelry. Anger in the town was fanned, and since no compromise was offered the whole affair went at last to Quarter Sessions, where the duke was, to his chagrin, defeated.

The inn's most prosperous days were, one imagines, those when barges were busily plying to and from London, and every bargee knew the most rewarding stopping places.

For centuries there had been talk of constructing a direct waterway between London and the south coast. Such a route had obvious advantages over the dreadful roads, and once established would be much cheaper to maintain. In addition it would be a lot shorter than the trip from the Thames right round the coast, and would not be exposed to the depredations of privateers or enemy men-of-war when we were in conflict with some European power, as we so often were.

Various schemes were mooted, and a number of bills introduced into Parliament. In 1641 the idea of using the Arun was put forward, much of its profitability being estimated on the conveyance of local commodities such as chalk, corn and wood, and especially Wealden iron and oak, both in demand for building and arming ships, and both almost impossible to carry by road during winter.

Little support was forthcoming during the Civil War, and in spite of a revival of interest after the Restoration it was not until the American War of Independence had begun that any real steps were taken.

There are three basic stages in the development of any such continuous waterway. First map out existing navigable rivers providing a not-too-tortuous route; where a river becomes too narrow, shallow or twisting, make a 'Navigation' by dredging and making cuts to by-pass the worst meanders; and then, where the whole thing peters out or goes off at a tangent, study the shortest distance to the next navigable river which might be linked to it by a man-made canal.

Since Norman times there had been successive campaigns to keep the Arun negotiable between town and sea. In 1785 the Arun Navigation Company started to dredge and straighten out the watercourse beyond Arundel towards Newbridge. Locks were installed, and a tunnel was dug through Hardham Hill and under Stane Street to eliminate the twists and turns of the river near Pulborough. At Orfold an aqueduct carried a section of canal over the river itself. All this was achieved by 1790.

On its own it was not enough. The ideal would be to join the Arun to the River Wey in Surrey, which had been canalised in the middle of the previous century as part of a scheme to foster trade between Guildford and London. At one point only 15 miles separated the navigable sections of the two waterways, and once linked they would provide the often debated thoroughfare from the capital to the sea.

By 1810 the third Earl of Egremont, already owner of the Rother Navigation and anxious to exploit wider outlets for the lead, marble and agricultural produce of his Petworth estates, decided to take a hand in the project. He and other local landowners issued a prospectus, presented a bill to Parliament, and were able to begin work in July 1813.

The junction canal took just over three years to complete. It ran 18 miles from Newbridge on the Arun to Shalford on the Wey, climbing and descending through some of the loveliest Sussex and Surrey countryside, by a series of 23 locks. There was great ceremonial on opening day, and great optimism about profits to come.

In fact it made a poor start, and although trade gradually picked up it was mainly a local trade. Shippers from London were reluctant to send consignments to Littlehampton when there was little chance of taking on a full load for the return journey. The locks slowed the traffic, and there was a whole range of tolls to be paid. For any extension of the journey, freight still had to be transhipped to coastal vessels. And, with the Napoleonic wars well and truly over, the dangers of direct sea passage had abated.

It was decided that business might improve if a direct link could be provided with the prosperous harbour and naval dockyards of Portsmouth. Another canal was therefore started, duly linking the Arun near Stopham bridge with Portsmouth via Thorney Channel and Langstone Harbour. A spur was added in the form of a ship canal from Hunston to Chichester. It was an expensive failure. Despite an upsurge of trade between 1830 and 1840, the whole system had been devised too late. Better roads were providing stiff competition, and even more deadly was the threat of the iron road. Within a few decades the great web of railway lines spun across the country would put the barges and terminals of even the more important industrial canals out of business.

One after another the companies were wound up. The Wey and Arun closed in 1871. The Rother Navigation, though abandoned, was for some reason not formally written off until 1936.

The locks crumbled, lock cottages were deserted, the banks subsided. Bridges were demolished. The railway company decided to fill in the section of Hardham tunnel where their lines crossed it. Many parts of the canal bed were levelled up and became agricultural land, or were built over.

After a century of neglect, attempts are being made to preserve or renew some stretches for recreational purposes. On the Wey and Arun, up to 80 or 100 volunteers at a time spend week-ends and holidays tearing at the undergrowth, removing trees and other obstructions, and clearing locks

and towpaths. Several miles have so far been liberated with
the aid of tractors and earth-moving equipment, some presented to the preservation trust, and some on loan. There
are plans to use electric pumps for 'recycling' water coming
down through the locks back up to the summit again.

Between Arundel and the junction, the river has reverted
to its old meandering ways, sometimes placid and reflective,
sometimes in turbulent flood. Amberley Wild Brooks can be
a network of meandering streams, or a great sheet of water,
giving the village itself the air of some transplanted fishing
port.

The castle here was developed from a palace built for the
bishops of Chichester after the see had been transferred from
Selsey. It was fortified by Bishop Rede in the fourteenth
century. Although his great hall and much else of the
building fell into ruin after the sixteenth century the gatehouse and castellated walls still make an impressive sight,
and shelter a more modestly proportioned, less aggressive
manor house.

Facing Amberley across the river is the agreeable little
village of Bury, dangerously close to a busy main road yet
somehow still private, not to say secretive. It has all that
it ought to have: church, duckpond, pub, and peace. John
Galsworthy lived and worked here when it must have been
even less ruffled that it is today.

But instead of wandering off in that direction, we must
follow the Arun back to the sea and to what lies east of
Littlehampton.

The return to the coast is disconcerting. Rustington and
Angmering are unassuming holiday places because, to
paraphrase a certain statesman's remark on a colleague, they
have a lot to be unassuming about. There is sand at low tide,
and beach and sea are both pleasant and safe for children.
Off season, when the children are gone, life is kept going
by a fair proportion of retired citizens. More than that one

cannot say with any fervour. Rustington seems the oddest of places in which to envisage the unstable genius of the great ballet dancer, Nijinsky; yet it was here that he came in January 1950. Cared for by his wife Romola through all the years of mental disturbance and insecurity since his collapse in 1918, he faced the prospect of homelessness once more when the lease of their house in Surrey expired. From Rustington a perfect stranger who had heard of their plight telephoned to offer them the hospitality of his home. Nijinsky knew a few months of contentment here before, on a visit to London, he fell ill and died.

Between the older part of Angmering and Poling, remains of a Roman villa were found which gave every indication of being more splendid than the Bignor discoveries; but the site is now buried under farmland beside a golf course.

Ferring and Goring run together. Goring, like Rustington, once offered shelter and the hope of recovery to a sick and despairing man of great talent. In April 1885 Richard Jefferies came to Sussex in the hope that a change of air might improve his health, and at first tried Crowborough. Many of his essays in *The Open Air* bring vividly to life Brighton, Beachy Head and downland as he saw them, and there are other loving studies in some of the posthumous volumes. The air of Crowborough, unhappily, proved rather too open and too bleak, and finally he settled at Goring in a house called banally but accurately 'Sea View', now renamed 'Jefferies' House'.

His writings here are filled with awareness of approaching death. He could no longer get about the countryside as he had loved to do. In his last essay he lamented:

No one else seems to have seen the sparkle on the brook, or heard the music at the hatch, or to have felt back through the centuries; and when I try to describe these things to

them they look at me with stolid incredulity . . . so that
perhaps after all I was mistaken, and there never was any
such place or any such meadow, and I was never there.
And perhaps in course of time I shall find out also, when I
pass away physically, that as a matter of fact there never
was any earth.

He died in August 1887. Goring today might not appeal to
him, but if his ghost has the power to explore our world it
will find that the earth on the Downs and far back into the
luxuriant Weald has not passed away, that the things and
places he saw are still there for those with eyes to see; and
that he was not mistaken.

Jefferies lies in Broadwater cemetery, Worthing. His
fellow naturalist and great admirer, W. H. Hudson, longed
to be buried near by but had to settle for a plot some 40 or
50 yards away. When he died in 1922 his stone was, by his
own wish, an exact copy of Jefferies' marble cross.

Behind Ferring, on Highdown Hill, the National Trust cares
for a remarkably complex archaeological site. Excavations
between 1892 and 1894 had revealed 86 graves of a Saxon
cemetery within the rampart of an early hill fort. Further in-
vestigations in this century showed that the fort, though used
during the third century A.D., came from the Early Iron Age,
and that below it again was a Bronze Age settlement. Not
far away down the slope is a Roman bath-house. A more
contemporary attraction is the garden laid out in a soft
undulation of rock plants and flowering shrubs, open to the
public all year round.

Wars with France encouraged not only an interest in the
inland waterways and a shift of coastal traffic to improving
roads, but also the expansion of the aristocratic tourist trade
within Britain itself. Deprived of the Grand Tour and of all
the spas and splendours of Europe, well-to-do holidaymakers

sought solace in the English watering-places, which hurried to adapt to their needs. What her brother, the Prince of Wales, was doing for Brighton, and her sister Charlotte was soon to do for Bognor, Princess Amelia did for Worthing. Her visit in 1798 gave the town the essential seal of royal favour, and from then on it developed rapidly. Population at the time could not have been more than a few thousand: when the first census was taken in 1801, the entire region between here and Angmering mustered only about 4,500. Today Worthing alone has some 85,000 residents, swollen out of all proportion during the summer season. In 1966 a report on the coast prepared by West Sussex County Council stated that a top priority was 'to increase the dwindling unspoilt coastline' and 'prevent any further pillaging of the coast by new development'. One must surely be in fervent agreement with this. But with more than 20 million holiday-makers rushing to the coast each year, of whom a more than manageable share opt for the shores of Kent and Sussex, what is to be done? Speculative builders and tycoons of the entertainment and accommodation industries seem always to have powers to override conservationists.

One entertainment which flourished early in Worthing was that of the theatre. Like most other actor-managers of his time, Mr Thomas Trotter depended for employment on an itinerant life, taking his troupe of strolling players from one town to another and giving performances in makeshift premises. His company's first recorded performance in Worthing was presented in a barn in the High Street, in 1802. Barns were quite commonly adapted for such dramatic ventures – hence the name of 'barn-stormer' for a strolling player – and Worthing at the turn of the century was able to guarantee a three-month season annually, three nights a week. The smarter residents and visitors following in Princess Amelia's footsteps, however, began to feel that such premises left much to be desired, and petitioned for a more suitable playhouse to be built. In 1807 Mr. Trotter was able to open his new theatre in Ann Street at a cost of £11,000, with Mr and Mrs Siddons playing the leading roles in *The Merchant of Venice* – not, as many a Worthing drama devotee wistfully likes to believe, Mrs Sarah Siddons, but her daughter-in-law.

The season was extended, to last from July to October. Programmes were lengthy, often with two or three plays a night, interpersed with sketches or musical items. Four hours was regarded as reasonable value for money, though many performances went on long after that.

Originally called the New Theatre, this admirably designed playhouse became the Theatre Royal in 1817, by which time Trotter, now a figure of some consequence, had also taken over the Brighton Theatre at a time when its reputation had been brought low by a series of slipshod productions, defaulting managers, and what a local newspaper called 'improvident speculations'. Trotter redecorated the theatre and raised the standard of performance, but there were difficulties, and after a benefit night in 1819 he relinquished control and continued in Worthing, living in an attractive villa which he had built beside the theatre, until his death in 1851.

His property was put up for auction, but his widow would not allow the buildings to be disposed of during her lifetime, as she had heard a rumour that one bidder wanted to use the theatre as a warehouse, and she did not propose to spend her remaining years 'next to a bacon and cheese store'. Attempts were made to keep the dramatic tradition alive under various managements, but attendance dropped off. One bleak November the theatre was 'opened for one night by an indifferent company to a worse audience'. On 6 December 1855 the curtain fell for the last time; and on 12 December Mrs Trotter died. A year later the executors sold the theatre for £160, the villa for £240.

13   The Seven Sisters, seen from Cuckmere Haven

Although the main building was used for much of its subsequent life as a warehouse, neither exterior nor interior was much altered, and in the 1960s a local amateur dramatic company erected and painted their scenery in it. Then in 1968 came the announcement that the theatre and Trotter's old home were to be demolished as part of a modern re-development scheme. A protest group was formed, with the backing of Sir John Betjeman, to urge the theatre's retention as an attractive oasis in any new building complex. The appeal came too late. Plans had been made and nobody had any intention of revising them.

Today there is no theatre in Ann Street.

The coast road here is dismal, and although the parallel road through Sompting is lapped by bungalows and semi-detached boxes flowing out from Worthing, at least it is suddenly enlivened by the famous Saxon tower of its church. This four-gabled cap with the angles meeting at the apex is known as a Rhenish helm, and is the only one of its kind in Britain. The body of the church is partly Norman and partly Early English. In 1154 the church was granted to the Knights Templar, who built a square chapel on the south side, a feature which still exists.

Another remarkable edifice soon rears up north of the road, perhaps seen best when approaching from the opposite direction. Its Gothic extravagance of pinnacles and buttresses has a lot in common with the cathedral at Arundel; and, like that, it is a product of Victorian romanticism. Lancing College was founded in 1848 by Nathaniel Woodard, at that time curate of New Shoreham, as one of a federation of Church of England schools which would unite all social classes in a common system of education. By the time of his death in 1891 there were 15 of these supposedly comprehensive public schools, including Ardingly and Hurstpierpoint.

The chapel at Lancing was begun in 1868. All the stone used in its construction was quarried by one family from

14 Net shops, Hastings

diggings belonging to the college at Scaynes Hill. Its appearance dates from 1911, by which time the advisability of adding the tower which had been part of the original plan was being wisely questioned. Even as it stands now, the soaring 94-foot-high chapel has demanded abnormally deep-sunk foundations, and the weight of a tower could prove catastrophic. It is unlikely that one will ever be provided now.

The efficacy of the founder's doctrines may be studied by the cynical in the early sections of Evelyn Waugh's recently published diaries.

Below the college on its commanding slope, the River Adur flows down from its source near Horsham to the sea, passing on its way only two towns of any consequence: Steyning and the stronghold from which the Rape takes its name, Bramber.

Steyning is one of several towns which refuse to be assigned to any particular segment of Sussex. It was once, like Arundel on the Arun, a port, but has long since ceased to retain anything but the faintest tang of the sea and its ways. In all moods and all weathers it is dominated by Chanctonbury Ring yet, lying in a cleft in the Downs, does not belong to them. Nor, in spite of its closeness to the edge of the Weald, is it a characteristic Wealden settlement. It remains independent, with its little gardens, its flint, brick and timber, its mellow roof tiles, Georgian doorways and its awesome church preserving so many Norman features, including the great chancel arch.

The first church here was built by St Cuthman, an eighth-century shepherd who brought his invalid mother on a cart from the west country. When it broke down in Steyning, he took this as an omen, stayed here, and is buried here.

Another religious figure associated with Steyning is the thirteenth-century anchorite Miliana, who proved to be a far from meek recluse. It was the vocation of an anchorite to shun the world and its temptations and to live in austere solitude, never leaving the cell and often being walled up in it after death. Many of these cells were set against the outer wall of a church, with a squint through which the occupant might follow the service. Food and cash donations came from local landowners and parishioners, and any surplus was a welcome addition to the priest's or bishop's income. Miliana, however, found it hard to detach herself altogether from the world. She must have spent a lot of her time in her cell brooding rather than meditating. In 1272 she somehow or other got round her vow of lifelong seclusion and emerged to sue another anchorite, Richard of Hardham, for rents which she claimed he had wrongly acquired. At the same time she sued the prior of Hardham for 5,600 loaves, 6,800 gallons of ale, and 5,600 messes which had been illegally withheld from her for 18 years. She seems to have won her case, but there is no record of the outcome. As L. F. Salzman observed many years ago in *Sussex Notes and Queries*, 'One wonders what would have happened if the prior had admitted his liability and dumped the whole lot outside her cell'.

The escarpment of neighbouring Bramber is spiky with the remaining wall of the Norman castle which once kept sur-veillance over the river. For more than five centuries it was the property of the dukes of Norfolk, until presented in 1946 to the National Trust. Much of the damage inflicted on it and never made good came from a bombardment during the Civil War.

Defoe, travelling through these parts, found Steyning a tolerable little market town, but thought Bramber hardly deserved to be classified as a town, 'having not above fifteen or sixteen families in it, and of them not many above asking you an alms as you ride by'. Yet in those corrupt days of rotten and pocket boroughs, its worth to parliamentary can-didates was such that 'it is said, there was in one king's reign more money spent at elections, than all the lands in the parishes were worthy, at twenty years purchase'.

Until a few years ago there was a remarkable museum in Bramber. Walter Potter, a Victorian taxidermist, constructed a number of tableaux from stuffed rabbits, squirrels and guinea-pigs, his masterpiece being a dramatic representation of the Death of Cock Robin. Taken over and removed to Brighton, it failed to attract enough paying customers and may be in danger of disappearing, unless salvaged for the ambitious toy collection now being assembled in the town. Its old home in Bramber is now a museum of pipes, advertising itself as 'the world's largest collection of smokiana', illustrating the evils and consolations of tobacco smoking. Among the exhibits are one from South America believed to be over a thousand years old, and a more recent one used by Stanley Baldwin.

The Adur reaches the sea at Shoreham and Southwick. The port, after a spell of depression, is now brisk again, trying to maintain a balance between holiday resort facilities and the usual quayside and light industrial clutter, all overtopped by huge power stations. When Old Shoreham harbour clogged up in the eleventh century, the town was stranded a mile inland, to be gradually replaced by New Shoreham. St Nicholas's church in the older town has some fine Norman work, but its restoration during this century makes it of less striking appeal than the 'new' town's St Mary de Haura (St Mary of the Harbour). Although this, too, has been much restored, mainly in the nineteenth century after crumbling to the verge of ruin, the remaining choir of the original church retains splendid Norman carving.

Marlipins, once a Customs storehouse, now a museum, has a wall of chequered flint and Caen stone remarkably resembling the decorative flushwork of East Anglia, little practised in the south despite the similarity of materials available.

There have been some royal comings and goings through

this harbour. King John landed here from France after the death of his brother, Richard Coeur-de-Lion, and within a few weeks of being crowned was on his way out again to defend his French possessions, in which he failed wretchedly. In 1651 King Charles II, unceremoniously and with even bleaker prospects, left via Southwick.

When news of his father's execution reached him in France, the young prince had proclaimed himself king, and in the following year landed in Scotland in the hope of re-establishing the monarchy. On 3 September 1651 he was defeated by Cromwell at the battle of Worcester, but escaped into hiding. For six weeks he wandered from one loyal friend to another, in spite of the price on his head and the watchfulness of those who longed to get their hands on him.

Attempts to spirit Charles away to the Continent from the west country having failed, his faithful companion Lord Wilmot decided it would be safer to try embarking from the Sussex coast. Colonel Gaunter of Runcton agreed to find a boat, and finally recommended Brighton. He escorted his king across the country from the Hampshire border, avoiding strong Puritan contingents. There was a nasty moment in Arundel when they came almost face to face with the Roundhead governor of the castle, but they escaped recognition. Then at Bramber they had to pass through a large number of soldiers, none of whom paid any attention whatsoever.

Charles was recognised in Brighton by the landlord of the inn where they waited for darkness and the tide, who insisted on kissing his hand. The skipper who had contracted to smuggle out two gentlemen fleeing justice after fighting an illicit duel also recognised the king, and at once increased the fare, asked that his boat should be insured, and went home to put on a clean shirt, which not unnaturally aroused his wife's suspicions. But on the night of 17 October Charles was at last safely aboard the lugger *Surprise* off the eastern bank of the harbour, on his way to an exile from which he would not return until after Cromwell's death.

When he did come back into his kingdom in 1660, the skipper who had saved him, Tattersell, lost no time in claiming his reward. He sailed up the Thames flying all the bunting he could cram on, and with his ship's name repainted as *The Royal Escape*. The hint appears to have been taken, for Tattersell was given various naval appointments, from which he was duly dismissed on grounds of misbehaviour, and from 1663 onwards was granted a pension. He bought what is now the Old Ship, Brighton's oldest inn, and became High Constable of Brighton, in which capacity he lost no opportunity of harassing Quakers and other Nonconformists. When he died in 1674 he and his wife were commemorated by a tombstone with a floridly congratulatory inscription conceived possibly by his son, possibly by himself. In spite of the favours he had received, the closing lines declare:

> *Since earth could not reward the worth him given,*
> *He now receives it from the King of Heaven.*
> *In the same chest one jewel more you have,*
> *The partner of his virtues, bed, and grave.*

From Southwick eastwards there is now no break in the streets and terraces. But gradually those terraces become more imposing, and at last we are bowling along the front at Hove and then Brighton – though it is not only football fans who automatically hear the names the other way round, as Brighton and Hove.

*   *   *

It was Brighton which, from the eighteenth century onwards, set the pattern for this coastline. Other resorts might consciously aspire to be more genteel, or might strike out in the opposite direction in search of vulgar profits. But here was the originator, arrogant to start with, later trying to make the best of both worlds.

The fishing village appears in Domesday Book as Bristel-mestune. By Defoe's time it had become Bright Helmston, 'commonly called Bredhemston', and in his view was unlikely to survive long, needing sturdier defence against the encroaching sea, 'the expense of which . . . will be eight thousand pounds which if one were to look on the town would seem to be more than all the houses in it are worth'.

Later prosperity is generally attributed to Dr Richard Russell of Lewes, who wrote a treatise on the salubrious effects of sea bathing and settled in Brighton in 1750 to promulgate his theories. In fact such pleasures and treatments had been practised for some considerable time before this. In 1736 the rector of Buxted, spending a holiday by the sea, wrote to a friend:

We are now sunning ourselves upon the beach
at Brighthelmstone, and observing what a
tempting figure this island must have been
in the eyes of those gentlemen who were
pleased to take the trouble of civilising
and subduing us. . . . My morning's business
is bathing in the sea, and then buying fish;
and my evening occupation is riding out for
air, viewing the old Saxon camps, and counting
the ships in the road and the boats that are
trawling. . . . the coast is safe, and the
cannons all covered with rust and grass, the
ships moored, no enemy apprehended.

Nevertheless it has to be conceded that it was Russell whose *Dissertation Concerning the use of Sea Water in Diseases of the Glands* brought a growing number of visitors to the town, to undergo a solemn ritual of immersion, assisted (sometimes forcibly) by muscular 'bathers' for the men and 'dippers' for the women.

Of all these visitors the key figure – a figure growing more bulbous and more grotesque as time went on – was that of the Prince of Wales, later Prince Regent, and ultimately King George IV.

George's first stay in Brighton was with his uncle, the Duke of Cumberland, during September 1783. In 1785 he secretly married the twice-widowed Mrs Fitzherbert, who took for herself a house in Brighton; and soon the prince was leasing a small farmhouse there, since until their marriage could be openly acknowledged his wife would not blatantly live under the same roof with him. Vowing to forswear his earlier dissipations, George soon found the little house too constricting, and set Henry Holland to work in 1787 on what was designated the Marine Pavilion of His Royal Highness. Holland tastefully transformed the house into a neo-classical villa.

In 1795, forced into an official marriage which proved a disaster, the prince renounced Mrs Fitzherbert, but was soon back with her. It was not until his father's madness necessitated his being appointed Prince Regent that the relationship was finally broken. During all these vicissitudes, George found most of his real happiness in Brighton, and, in defiance of his political detractors, the resentful general public, and perhaps his own doubts and frustrations, began to lavish money on his pavilion there. In 1803 stables were added to the villa in the form of a pseudo-eastern Dome which looked, commented Sydney Smith, as if the dome of St Paul's had come here and pupped. This, together with Holland's addition of some Chinese wallpaper within the villa itself, fired George's imagination. Nothing would suffice now but an Oriental setting.

Wyatt and Repton were both asked to submit ideas, but

in the end the shape and style of the expanded Pavilion were determined by John Nash, the prince's own favourite architect. Between 1815 and 1822 he created this incredible microcosm of Xanadu on the English Channel. Description of its treasures is futile: one has to walk through the rooms oneself, approving or laughing helplessly – sometimes both. When the Pavilion ceased to be a royal residence, much of its furniture was dispersed, along with paintings, fittings, and *objets d'art*, but after Brighton Corporation took it over in 1850 a great deal was returned on permanent loan by successive generations of the Royal Family. Most impressive is the great banqueting room with its chandelier and candelabra, its dragons and Chinese murals. At a time of depression and near-famine, the vast meals offered to the Prince Regent's guests provoked revolutionary feeling throughout the country; and certainly one has to marvel at the menu displayed in the vast kitchen, a menu which even the most ambitious deep-freeze restaurants of our own day would not dare to attempt.

The Pavilion grounds were illuminated in 1818 by gas from the new gasworks at Black Rock, and when chandeliers within the building were adapted, the Prince Regent and Nash came down from London to view the spectacle. In the following year gas was also piped to the Theatre Royal, its advantages being widely and fulsomely advertised by the management.

Mr Trotter, whom we have already met in Worthing, had reopened the playhouse, on the site of the present Theatre Royal, on 23 July 1814 under the patronage of His Royal Highness the Prince Regent. It could seat an audience of 1,400 and included, naturally, a special box for the town's royal patron, divided from other playgoers by richly gilded iron lattices. On his first playbill the new manager gave evidence of his solemn dedication to the tasks which lay ahead:

In adding the Brighton Theatre to his other
establishment (Worthing), Mr. Trotter feels
an additional stimulus to future exertion;
he is aware much, very much, is requisite to
restore that concern to its pristine
consequence, and, though by removing many
evils materially militating against the
respectability of this establishment, he may,
perhaps, subject himself to the censure of a
few, yet, he boldly asserts, that every new
arrangement is formed with the view of
ultimate comfort and respectability. As
has lately been the custom to promise much,
without strictly adhering to the performance,
Mr T. will say little on the score of scenic
decoration, wardrobe, etc. He cannot,
however, forbear observing, that no pieces
will be brought forward without the strictest
attention to every appointment requisite for
rendering them worthy notice – no expense has
been, or shall be spared, to ensure success.

Unfortunately the theatre was not as successful as his
Worthing venture had been, in spite of productions 'intended
as correctives to the vitiated qualities of our nature, by exhibiting vice in its repelling deformity, and the lovely superi-
ority of virtue, in all its impressive and dignified bearings',
and in spite of Trotter having wooed fashionable patrons
such as Princess Augusta, Mrs Fitzherbert, and the Dukes of
York, Clarence and Cumberland. After the end of his five-
year tenure his successor managed to lose so much money
that within just over a year he was forced to close and
auction off about £2,000-worth of scenery and wardrobe
for £67.

The fickle Prince Regent virtually deserted Brighton in

1827. Ten years later Mrs Fitzherbert died, and was buried in the church of St John the Baptist, where her memorial shows her left hand with three wedding rings on it.

Brighton's prosperity was well established by now. From the 1820s onwards it continued to expand rapidly. Kemp Town was originally meant to be almost a separate community, with its own town centre around Sussex Square, its own parish church, and its own shopping streets. It was conceived by Thomas Read Kemp, originator of a religious sect and of this concept of a high-class residential area cut off from the contamination of its neighbour. Poor Brighton! As is the way of such things, no sooner had it become both fashionable and prosperous than it was condemned by many of its own inhabitants, who set about moving out into less commercialised enclaves or, where these were not available, building them.

Kemp Town on one side was balanced by a proposed Brunswick Town on the other, built on land owned by a more orthodox clergyman than the dissenting Kemp. But Brunswick Town blurred into Hove, and the visitor may find difficulty in telling where one district ends and the next begins. Local residents have fierce loyalties and no such doubts. Only a few weeks before writing these pages I overheard a waitress in Brighton lamenting to a colleague, 'It gets worse every year – I don't know what I'd do if I couldn't go back to Hove every evening'.

Brighton may 'get worse every year' but it is still a sparkling town, a slightly swaggering town of indefinable style. Parking is a nightmare; walking, save along the spacious esplanade, a risky business. But there is always the traffic-free, if somewhat elbow-jostling, sanctuary of The Lanes. These narrow lanes or 'twittens' represent the original centre of the old town. Although most of them date only from the late eighteenth and nineteenth centuries, they were set out along the original pattern of the area between East Street and

West Street. Meeting House Lane is the longest and most attractive. The modern development of Brighton Square harmonises admirably without being in any way imitative. Yet a mere half century ago these streets were dismal and well-nigh forgotten. In 1926 they could be spoken of as 'poor old grandparents, whom the *nouveau riche* descendants find it convenient to ignore'. The kiss of reawakening was given by another royal visitor. Queen Mary, wife of King George v, was an avid antique hunter, and once she had found unsuspected riches in The Lanes the whole complex became fashionable. There are times when the modern stroller is tempted to wonder how, even after crowded centuries of history, there can *be* that many genuine antiques still for sale.

Now and then the interested collector may come across relics, in these shops, of what was once a busy and profitable trade in Brighton. Before the invention of photography there was quite a craze for silhouette portraits; and, in fact, many practitioners were so highly thought of that they continued to ply their craft well into the photographic era, up to the First World War.

The name of the process indicates scorn. It was the name of a French politician, Etienne de Silhouette, whose rigorous economies in financial administration became so closely associated with cheapness and austerity that it was applied mockingly to these cut-out substitutes for more lavishly detailed, painted miniatures. The minister and the slur are forgotten; the word is still with us. In Brighton, many dexterous artists set up studios early in the nineteenth century, advertising their skills without false modesty : one claimed to have been 'Profilist to the Royal Family at Windsor'. The National Portrait Gallery has, indeed, a fine example of the work of one local silhouettist, showing George iv and his brother Frederick, Duke of York. Another, who worked on the Chain Pier, suffered from deafness, and whatever was said to him would automatically reply, 'One and six, head and shoulders; two and six, full length'.

With the Sussex coastal resorts growing in popularity, something had to be done to make them more comfortably accessible. At the end of the eighteenth century, when road-building everywhere else in the country was improving apace, Arthur Young could still say of the best Sussex roads that it would be 'a prostitution of language to call them turnpikes'. Within a couple of decades, things had taken a turn for the better. At least, most people considered it was for the better. William Cobbett, always hostile to any further spread of the Great Wen of London, viewed with concern the growing population of City men taking advantage of the salubrious air of Brighton:

It is so situated that a coach which leaves it
not very early in the morning, reaches London
by noon. Great parcels of stock-jobbers stay
at Brighton, with the women and children. They
skip backwards and forwards on the coaches and
actually carry on stock-jobbing in Change Alley
though they reside at Brighton.

Cobbett was equally indignant about the way in which roads which had not been turnpiked were neglected. On a journey from Petworth to Lavant he wished to avoid going round by the turnpike through Chichester, but found that the innkeepers, ostlers and post boys with whom he had to deal could offer no assistance when it came to travelling by anything but the most obvious highways: 'They think you a strange fellow if you will not ride six miles on a turnpike road rather than two on any other road'.

The parallel between this and our present choice between motorways and country lanes is ironic. Cobbett should have considered himself lucky, as many a wise modern traveller does, that the majority of drivers are content to follow one another nose to tail along the turnpikes, leaving the true pleasures of the countryside to the more appreciative.

Not that everybody, even in those days, wished the county to be opened up by fast routes to the metropolis. When the first adequate highway from London to Brighton was mooted, residents of Hurstpierpoint petitioned for it to be diverted from their doorsteps, on the grounds that it would make it too easy for cut-throats and pick-pockets to come down from London and ply their trade locally. Let the roads stay muddy, perilous and uninviting!

By the 1840s there were more than 30 coaches running daily between London and Brighton, the average journey taking six hours, for a fare of 15 shillings. But the road passenger services, like the canal freight services, were threatened by a formidable rival. At a quarter to seven in the morning of Tuesday, 21 September 1841, a train left London and reached Brighton just after nine o'clock. It was the first of many, and fashioned the future not merely of Brighton but of all the coastal resorts.

During the boom of 'railway mania', competing companies made colourful claims regarding their ability to lay sound tracks on a sound basis, with a guarantee of sound dividends for investors. In 1835 Parliament had received six separate proposals for a line from London to Brighton. One of these, with the backing of Robert Stephenson, advocated a fairly trouble-free route cutting through the South Downs by the Adur gap and taking in Shoreham before looping east. Sir John Rennie's alternative suggestion was shorter but more expensive, involving a tunnel through the Downs below Clayton. The latter route was chosen, at an ultimate cost of £40,000 a mile, incorporating not merely the unavoidable tunnel but a superb viaduct 1,475 feet long and 96 feet high at its central section, to this day standing up to the added strain of increased electric traffic. Construction was threatened at one point when the railway navvies found themselves a couple of miles from the nearest source of beer and were on the verge of striking. It was speedily arranged that boys should be hired to fetch beer, for which they received one halfpenny a trip.

On Easter Monday 1844 the first excursion train from London to Brighton set out with 45 carriages drawn by four engines. It acquired extra loads during the journey, and on arrival sported 57 coaches and six engines. The day trip to the seaside was brought within the range of many who could not have afforded the time or cost of the stage coach; and even for those on a more leisurely route there came the burgeoning profits of the middle-class holiday of a seaside week or two.

In 1846 the London and Brighton Railway was incorporated with the London and Croydon line into the London, Brighton and South Coast Railway. Within these few years the number of daily coaches on the London to Brighton turnpike had diminished to one. The railways reached out to Bognor, to Hastings, and to Worthing, in a web of main and branch lines. Towns along the route flourished, and some, such as Hassocks and Haywards Heath, could almost be said to have been conceived and nurtured by the railways. Hove shudderingly resisted the idea of having a station at all for some time, and even by 1880 little enthusiasm was shown for an offer of reduced rate season tickets to and from London.

With a speeding up of trains, the line to Brighton became a commuters' line. The last representative of its very special glory, retained into the impersonal days of British Rail, was the prestigious Pullman train, the Brighton Belle. This was recently abolished on the grounds that it was not making money. As one critic observed, 'Anyone who could lose money on the Brighton Belle would have been capable of losing money on the invention of the wheel.'

Brighton has always attracted, inspired, and even given birth to, painters and writers. John Constable stayed here, largely in the hope of an improvement in his wife's health, and although he declared it 'the receptacle of the fashion and off-scouring of London' with 'nothing here for a painter', he painted some masterpieces in the locality, including some light-drenched beach scenes. Anna Sewell, lamed at the age of 16, moved here in the year of her accident and spent over 20 more years in Sussex, though it was not until she returned to her native Norfolk that she actually committed *Black Beauty* to paper. In 1872 Aubrey Beardsley was born in Brighton. His grammar school teachers were quick to recognise his artistic talents, and when he was 16 he was encouraged to provide the illustrations for the programme of the Christmas pantomime which the school staged in the Dome. He also took part in this musical entertainment himself, in company with a schoolfellow, C. B. Cochran, who in due course was to become even more of a theatrical figure.

In 1961 the University of Sussex was established in Stanmer Park, on the north-eastern outskirts of the town. It is not, in the current catch-phrase, a redbrick university: rather, concrete and red brick. When it came to introducing a wall of knapped flint in tribute to the county's historical and geological foundations, the architect, Sir Basil Spence, was dismayed to learn that there was no longer any craftsman in Sussex skilled in the working of the flint.

Three routes run parallel out of Brighton from the Palace Pier for about a mile and a half before converging on the large swimming pool and the multi-million-pound yacht marina now under construction at Black Rock. They are the Marine Parade, Madeira Drive, where the annual veteran car run from London finishes, and a jaunty little electric tramway commemorating the experiments of Magnus Volk.

Towards the end of the last century, Volk laid out an electric railway from Brighton, past Black Rock, to a jetty

15 The South Downs above Alfriston

below Rottingdean. The rails were set in concrete blocks below the sea, and power was provided through an overhead cable fed from a generating station at Rottingdean. Existing photographs show it as a sort of miniature oil rig packed with passengers, and it is not surprising that it was soon dubbed 'Daddy-long-legs'. The Mayor of Brighton opened the line on 29 November 1886. A week later it was badly damaged in a gale. Even in more clement weather it was not a great success, since even the gentlest waves slowed it down, and sand and shingle repeatedly clogged the rails.

Volk's invention lurched on into this century, but could not be kept in satisfactory working order. All that remains apart from its land-locked successor on less ambitious but less vulnerable lines is a hunk of concrete block here and there among the rocks, identifiable by the keen industrial archaeologist at low tide.

16 *Lewes Castle Barbican*

CHAPTER THREE

Black Rock to Cliff End

Looking down on the nave of Rottingdean's parish church of St Margaret from behind the pulpit is an impressive bust of Thomas Hooker, vicar from 1792 to 1838. He supplemented his private income by running a small private school in the vicarage, among his pupils being Bulwer Lytton, the novelist, and a boy who was to be converted to Roman Catholicism and become Cardinal Manning. It is fairly well established that Hooker made further profits from the local smuggling trade, acting as look-out when cargoes were being run ashore and hidden in the caves of the cliff face or in the tangle of subterranean passages of which traces still remain beneath the village High Street. As Rudyard Kipling lived here for a time, and had many family connections in the village, it seems reasonable to suppose that the jingle of 'Brandy for the Parson, Baccy for the Clerk' first stirred in his mind when contemplating, or later remembering, the austere countenance of the Reverend Hooker.

'Smuggling is the chief support of the inhabitants, in which they are very Dext'rous', reads an old history of the village, 'for which innocent and beneficial practise (sad to relate) Captain Dunk the Butcher paid £500 and ten of his worthy friends were lodged in Hawsham Jaol or in their elegant language were sent for a few months to colledge to improve their manners'. Beacon Hill was one of a chain of signal posts ordained by Henry VIII and used in Elizabethan times to warn of the approaching Spanish Armada; but when the smock mill was moved there in 1802 it was employed for signalling and warnings of a less patriotic kind – the set of its sails being adjusted to give messages to incoming smugglers and to hold them off if Preventive men were in the vicinity.

When thinking of smugglers we usually conjure up a romantic picture of the 'gentlemen' going by in the dark with spirits, tobacco and lace shipped in illicitly from France or the Netherlands. But long before this import business became so popular, south coast traders specialised in duty-free exports, primarily and most profitably of wool. Clothiers, tired of the stiff tariffs imposed supposedly for their own protection but really benefiting only the merchants of the staple towns, set about circumventing the royal duty collectors. If there had to be middlemen, they preferred hard-working rogues who took a fair commission to the bureaucrats and their crippling levies. From Edward I to Charles II restrictions on quantities which could be exported varied in severity; regulatory duties swung up and down, according to the economic theories of the time; and penalties for avoidance became lethal. Still the illicit trade flourished and was, deplorably, carried on with much greater efficiency than legitimate export business. In 1698 the authorities were notified by their own supervisor for Sussex and Kent that within a few weeks some 160,000 sheep would be shorn on Romney Marsh, and that the greater proportion of the fleeces would find their way swiftly to France. Strong forces of Revenue officers proved helpless against the stronger contingents of smugglers and their local accomplices. Armed bands patrolled the countryside and saw the precious cargoes safely afloat. The gangs contained many petty criminals and bully-boys, but their organisation was usually controlled by men of good standing. 'It is well known', lamented a seventeenth-century critic, 'that smugglers are not of meanest persons in the places where they dwell, but have oftentimes great interest with the magistrates; and, being purse-proud, do not value what they spend to ingratiate themselves with persons of authority, to distrust all such as discover their fraudulent dealings, or else by bribes to stop their mouths'.

Seaford's present training college for teachers was founded

on the dismantled materials of a building in Ringmer known as Corsica Hall, in tribute to the profits made from Corsican wine smuggled into this country.

The import smugglers appear to have been a tougher, more ruthless lot than the wool exporters. Pitched battles with Preventive men and the militia grew more frequent and more insolent, and there were savage attacks on individuals suspected, rightly or wrongly, of informing to the authorities. Even when local people disapproved of this spreading violence, they found it wise to keep quiet. Some continued to help readily, and received generous hand-outs. Others helped whether they liked it or not: many a farmer found himself short of labour on the farm because his hands were in more lucrative temporary employment, or found that his horses had been 'borrowed' for a night or two to assist in transporting tubs and bales from the beach to various hiding places. Innumerable churchyards, among them those of Pevensey and Broadwater, had their complement of sham graves which were really caches for contraband, and many a house retains with some pride its secret cupboards, passages and cellars.

A number of major storehouses and meeting places were far inland. Some locations, when examined, prove to be near rivers or tributaries up which small boats could be rowed at night. Others are deep in the woods, and one might think of these as being unnecessarily remote and dangerous: the further the goods had to be carried overland, the greater the opportunity for pursuers to catch up and pounce. But 'the foul ways of Sussex' were still a formidable hindrance to any large body of strangers – and the forces of law and order had to be strangers, since few local men would willingly serve against the powerful free-traders.

Most notorious and most violent of all were the Hawkhurst gang, who made their headquarters in that Kentish town just over the border although they were all Sussex men. In 1747 they had grown so bold that they mustered all available forces in a forest near Chichester and rode to Poole, where they smashed open the Custom House and made off with a great load of goods. It was a daring raid, and good for their reputation; but what followed turned the countryside against them. When one of their number was captured, other members of the gang waylaid two men travelling to Chichester to give evidence before the magistrates, and murdered them. One was thrown alive down a well and showered with heavy stones, the other whipped to death and buried on the Downs. The corpses were soon found, and the ring-leaders hunted down. Six men were hanged, and one awaiting execution died in prison.

The sight of corpses dangling from gibbets did not deter the fraternity. The remaining Hawkhurst men doubtless found it wise to lie low for a while, and then start trading under a different name. Stringent laws made no difference. Wars made no difference: unless, perhaps, unofficial trade actually intensified during the frequent periods when official trade between the perennially contentious France and England lapsed. Smugglers on both sides of the Channel had no qualms about 'consorting with the enemy'. The commerce was so blatant that Kent and Sussex, like the East Anglians, brazenly maintained resident agents in key centres abroad to do their buying and make shipping arrangements. In the late eighteenth century it was estimated that almost four million gallons of hollands gin were ordered in Schiedam alone, and millions of pounds of tea came in every year from France.

It would be difficult to make a landing undetected along this part of the shore today, and difficult at the best of times to cross the main road. Rottingdean, at first sight from that main road, appears to be just a segment of the Saltdean, Telscombe Cliffs and Peacehaven sprawl. But a hundred yards into the village itself, there are pleasant surprises waiting.

The old *Black Horse Inn* was here in Henry vııı's time. Its lounge was once a blacksmith's forge. *Whipping Post House* was a butcher's shop, and here lived that Captain Dunk whose associates had to spend some time in Horsham gaol repenting their misdemeanours, or planning fresh ones. Adjoining is the *Plough*, another inn of long tradition, which overlooks the wide pond and a fine medley of expansive house frontages, among them Thomas Hooker's old vicarage. This became a private residence shortly before the First World War and was bought by William Nicholson, the painter, who renamed it *The Grange*. It now houses the public library, some examples of Nicholson's work, and a fascinating toy museum.

This museum has an entrancing collection of British and foreign toys – rocking-horses, tops, penny toys from Victorian days and Noah's Arks of different ages and different degrees of sumptuousness, clockwork models, theatres and dolls' houses. There is also a special display of the best examples of modern toy-making. It is planned to transfer the museum eventually to Brighton, where it will be supplemented by further delights at the moment in store there, but for at any rate a couple of years the main collection will remain in Rottingdean.

Sir Edward Burne-Jones and his wife lived at North End House, and the artist contributed the designs from which William Morris made the glowing stained-glass windows for the tower and chancel of St Margaret's church. The east window was Sir Edward's personal gift to commemorate his daughter Margaret's wedding. Lady Burne-Jones was a great character in her own right, and caused uproar in the village when she greeted news of the relief of Mafeking by hanging out a banner which read: 'We have killed and also taken possession'.

Husband and wife are buried in the churchyard close to their granddaughter Angela Thirkell, the novelist. Lady Burne-Jones's nephew was Rudyard Kipling, who lived for some time at The Elms, leaving only when autograph hunters and other persecutors grew too persistent. Kipling's cousin, Stanley Baldwin, is also remembered here: a chair in the sanctuary of St Margaret's was presented in 1942 to mark the fiftieth anniversary of his wedding.

A less earnest occupant of the churchyard is G. H. Elliott, the music hall entertainer always billed as 'The Chocolate-Coloured Coon'.

North End House was bought in 1923 by Sir Roderick Jones, no relation of its earlier owners. His wife Enid Bagnold's best-selling novel, *National Velvet*, has a setting with marked resemblances to Rottingdean.

The church has a few traces of Saxon work, the village itself being the Saxon dene or vale of Rota's people. A tower which must have been too weighty for its supports was put up by the Normans, but collapsed in a gale and brought a lot of the church down with it. The present tower dates from A.D. 1200. Dedication to St Margaret was a result of the First Crusade, when the legend of this saint was brought back from the east at the same time as that of St George. Both are conventionally shown slaying a dragon with a sword or the base of a cross, or, as in the radiant window here, standing with one foot upon the defeated creature.

Above Rottingdean the road climbs through Ovingdean and Woodingdean towards flinty Falmer and the main Brighton to Lewes road. Ovingdean's churchyard shelters William Willett, who must turn uneasily in his grave if he hears the contumely now so often poured upon his literally enlightened notion of daylight-saving-time. The altar panels within are the work of William Morris, displaying an undeniable affinity with the windows which he and Burne-Jones created for Rottingdean. There is an old tale, of little substance, that Charles II passed through the village on his way to Brighton and, ultimately, Shoreham. Roundabout as his route may have been, this would surely have been absurdly circuitous. Harrison Ainsworth used the theme in his novel

Ovingdean Grange, which has not stood the test of time as well as some of his other romances.

This and its following villages belong to the Downs, and we are for the moment committed to the coast, which means we must hurry through Saltdean (who would wish to linger there?) and on towards Newhaven.

Here we meet the next of the divisive Sussex rivers, the Ouse. Rising near Crawley, it comes down past the obligatory castle at Lewes to a harbour whose 'new'-ness dates from the late sixteenth century. Before that, the river turned below Meeching Down and ran eastwards, parallel with the coast, into Seaford. Then severe flooding and raging storms diverted it through Meeching, which duly became Newhaven.

The seventeenth-century *Bridge Hotel* was the first refuge of Louis Philippe and his queen after the 1848 Revolution in France. It stands today on a twist of the road approaching the swing bridge over the bustling harbour. I say that it stands, but I would never be surprised to learn that it had overnight been shaken to dust by the pounding of traffic. Newhaven's prosperity began with coal traffic and mounted when the railway company took over the harbour, deepening the tideway and completing the installation of the swing bridge by 1867. Passenger services to Dieppe were added to the foreign and coastal freight trade: in the middle of the nineteenth century 40,000 passengers a year were carried; by the end of the century there were five times this number, while goods traffic had increased more than five and a half times. Today the car ferries add to the congestion, the traffic diversions are diverting in one sense only, and no driver can contemplate with any enjoyment the all-too-familiar prospect of being trapped in a jam on either side of that bridge. Yet Newhaven manages, with no visual charm and few social graces to commend it, to be an energetic, enlivening muddle of a place rather than an exasperating one.

Which is more than can be said for Seaford. This deserted

port is really not worthy of its surroundings, which are magnificent. The Downs loom over it, the lovely vale of the river Cuckmere opens up to the east, and beyond is the Heritage Coast stretch designated by the Countryside Commission as an area of outstanding natural beauty, unforgettably supported on its seaward rim by the chalk cliffs of the Seven Sisters.

A corporate member of the Cinque Ports, Seaford claims the westernmost Martello tower in the chain which was strung out between here and the Suffolk coast when Napoleon threatened to invade. William Pitt the Younger, then Lord Warden of the Cinque Ports and Prime Minister, ordered the construction of more than 70 towers along the south-east coast, and some were also set up on the Channel Islands. The prototype was a small fort in Martello Bay, Corsica, which held out for some time with only three cannon against a British Navy unit. It had to be attacked from the land, and before its demolition a number of plans were made of the design. Copies of these are on display in the Wish Tower, a Martello tower at Eastbourne which was restored and opened to the public in 1970.

The basic structure was that of a truncated cone just over 30 feet high, with an entrance high up the wall so that a ladder could be used and then hauled in, just as on church towers and other defences in the times of the Danish raids. The full complement of more than 100 forts was achieved long after the threat of invasion had subsided. Sussex had 47, the farther end of its barricade being at Rye Harbour. This tower, like a few others, was supplemented by a concentric outer wall enclosing a dry moat. The Rye Harbour example, though decrepit and unlikely to benefit from the proximity of a caravan park, is still in good enough shape to display the salient features.

Cobbett's easily fanned indignation burned up at the mere sight of these expensive relics in 1823 :

To think that I should be destined to behold
these monuments of the wisdom of Pitt and
Dundas and Perceval! ... I think I have
counted upwards of thirty of these ridiculous
things along here, which, I dare say, cost
five, perhaps *ten*, thousand pounds each; and
one of which was, I am told, *sold* on the coast of
Sussex, the other day, for TWO HUNDRED
POUNDS! ... All along the coast there are
works of some sort of other; incessant
sinks of money; walls of immense
dimensions; masses of stone brought and put
into piles. Then you see some of the walls
and buildings falling down; some that have
never been finished. ...

Contemporary parallels are not hard to come by.

Not that defence against the French was in itself a thing to
be sneered at. In one year alone, 1377, French raiders had
burned Rottingdean, destroyed churches in Hastings, and
sacked Rye and made off with its church bells. Watchbell
Street in Rye took its name from the warning which was all
too often sounded there when attack from the sea was immi-
nent. Over the centuries, smugglers might maintain a happy
liaison through peace and war; but other rogues, with or
without their government's blessing, indulged in hit-and-run
raids or extended piratical exercises.

The *Sussex Weekly Advertiser*, first weekly newspaper to
be published in the county, reported on 5 September 1796
the capture of a French privateer, *Petit Diable*, off Fairlight
by a revenue cutter which had already seized two others in
the preceding fortnight:

On Wednesday morning one of those petty
depredators landed several men within a mile

of Hastings where they proceeded to fill
their water-casks with the greatest
deliberation, and having got them on board
again steered their vessel close alongshore
and at the distance of about two miles from
the spot where the men had landed, captured
an English brig. A cutter was speedily
manned from Hastings and after a short
pursuit, recaptured the brig, and carried
her into Rye Harbour.

The writer felt that more cruisers should be stationed in the Channel to protect our legitimate traders from this harassment. He also regretted that Captain Amos, of the admirable revenue cutter, was not getting the perks which were his due since, it seemed, 'the expenses attending to their condemnation have been very nearly equal to his share of prize money'. If a little more financial encouragement were to be offered in such cases, still greater energy might conceivably be injected into the service.

Two weeks later the newspaper had to report the appearance of another impertinent raider off Seaford. As there was no official vessel within range, Lord Berkeley insisted on putting to sea in his own yacht with a hastily mustered crew of local guardsmen; but the surf was so high that the yacht was unable to get under weigh before the enemy had dashed off.

In July 1797 the body of a sailor who had apparently been slashed in several places by some sharp weapon and then shot through the head was brought ashore by the tide near Worthing, and there buried. The corpse was later exhumed and identified by a son and nephew as that of a sloop master named Brooker. His vessel, the *Happy Return* of Newhaven, had been captured by a French privateer but soon re-taken, to make at any rate a relieved return to Shoreham. It was, however, without its master: Brooker had been murdered aboard his own ship because he refused to surrender his watch and money without a fight. The remains were re-interred in Broadwater churchyard.

*   *   *

The Cuckmere was never regarded by the Normans or by anyone else as one of the strategic rivers of the county. Rising near Heathfield, it ambles its unpretentious way past Hellingly and Hailsham to Alfriston, and then on to the sea through a valley which it seems not so much to have carved out as absent-mindedly, erratically picked out during its meandering progress. Streams and marshy patches make walking on its wide levels tricky, but there are reliable tracks along either side of the valley. It is no place for anyone in a hurry. The road carries a booming procession of traffic over Exceat Bridge; but it is not difficult to turn one's back on it and, though perhaps never getting quite out of earshot, at least to relegate it to a murmuring distance.

This is the last stretch of coastal walking or driving to be had for six miles or so. Here the Downs take command right to the water's edge. Between Cuckmere Haven and Birling Gap are the chalky faces and undulating brows of the Seven Sisters – Haven Brow, Short Brow, Rough Brow, Bran Point, Flagstaff Point, Bail's Hill, and Went Hill Brow. These beautiful ladies and the green hair on their incomparable heads are now, it is hoped, shielded from all man-made ills. Sections of cliff and downland came under the National Trust at various times from 1928 onwards, and now with the classification of the whole area as one of outstanding natural beauty it should surely be safe from the indignities inflicted on other such charmers.

A twisting road manages to find its way back to the coast for a momentary glimpse of Birling Gap, whose natural cleft was once an excellent reception point for smuggled goods.

The smugglers used steps cut into the sheer chalk. Today there is a skeletal contrivance of scaffolding and steps down to the shore, a mosaic of chalk smears, green flints, green-slimed rocks and muddy sand. The few local fishing-boats still plying a trade here have to be hauled vertically up the cliff.

To the east is the old Belle Tout lighthouse, and beyond it the familiar, much photographed red and white column of the lighthouse below Beachy Head. The name of this headland, 570 feet high, has nothing to do with the beach at its foot, but is a corruption of the Norman French *Beau Chef*.

Packed as it may be with parked cars, its summit is still awe-inspiring. The Downs roll away to the north and west, and white-hemmed blue water sketches the curve of coast towards Bexhill and Hastings in the east. Such wide expanses of land and sea can never, even on the calmest day, be exactly the same for a few minutes at a time: cloud shadows vie with swathes of sunlight over the sweeping pasture and cornland, and race across the water; distant hotels and apartment blocks sharpen and then recede, trim little model kits or just white blobs in a shimmering haze.

'Eastbourne', says a doctor of my acquaintance, 'is a paradise for undertakers'. Certainly the panorama of the town from above takes in one of the largest cemeteries I can remember having seen. From the beginning of its expansion in Victorian times, Eastbourne made it clear that it had no intention of competing with Brighton or any other resort in the neighbourhood. Its holiday traffic has increased in this century, and contributes to the town's welfare; yet even now it belongs to its residents more than to its visitors, however lavish their spending. Old Eastbourne offers little of great historical or architectural interest. New Eastbourne is a clean, bright, spacious arrangement of large hotels, middle-sized hotels, and little residential hotels, in each of which it is hard not to visualise a scene from a Terence Rattigan play being performed twice nightly and several times a day.

The shops are good, there are some good restaurants – in many of which the regulars, proprietors and staff are on friendly terms varying in respectfulness and effusiveness which utterly exclude the stranger – and three good theatres conveniently situated with a few yards of each other. The regulars are easily identifiable in the audiences here, too. There is a preponderance of well-groomed ladies with silver hair or blue rinses, whose husbands have retired here and/or died. The best orchestras come; ballet and opera come; there is an adventurous choice of drama. There is in fact only one word for it, applicable in both its popular and its correct meanings, and without condescension : Eastbourne is a *nice* place.

For the visitor foreign to the town, one place which deserves a visit and which probably gets few from the residents is the Royal National Lifeboat Museum, exhibiting types of lifeboat from the earliest to the most recent, together with all the relevant equipment. Beside it is the Coastal Defence Museum in the Martello tower known as the Wish Tower. This offers no suggestion that you should throw coins in a fountain or a well : the 'wish' or 'wash' is Old English for a marshy area.

Such plebeian entertainments and amusements as there are tend to group around the eastern end of the town, and the standard of accommodation peters out into a scattering of bungalows and chalets near the Crumbles.

This depressingly named stretch of shingle reaching almost into Pevensey has been the scene of two brutal murders. The only thing to be said in their favour is that they took place so far from the respectable part of Eastbourne.

On a sunny day in August 1920, a little boy playing on the Crumbles tripped over a human foot which was sticking up out of the shingle. When uncovered, the body was identified by an Eastbourne landlady as that of a 17-year-old typist who had been spending a holiday at her boarding-house. She had been seen a number of times in the company of two attentive young men. It is an ordinary enough situation: the pretty young holidaymaker picked up by two admirers, flirting and perhaps going too far, perhaps refusing to go too far. By now the girl was no longer pretty. Her face and head had been smashed in with a large brick which still lay near by.

The two men, Jack Field and William Gray, were found and questioned. They tried to persuade another girl friend to provide them with an alibi, but she hurriedly left the district, and they were arrested and charged. Gray, who proved to be married, tried while in prison awaiting trial to establish another alibi, even more inept than the first.

Nevertheless they had the best defence they could have hoped for in court. Gray was represented by the famous Marshall Hall, who cast doubts on the medical evidence regarding time of death, and poured scorn on the idea that a girl could have been murdered in broad daylight and buried in the shingle without anyone noticing. His skill did not save his client. Both men were found guilty. On appeal they contradicted each other, and then each set about trying to accuse the other of the crime. Marshall Hall himself admitted later that, while doing his best for the defence, he had hoped throughout that they would hang. They did.

There was another murder, in one of the bungalows, in 1924. On this occasion the victim was chopped into gory pieces by her lover. Later tenants of the property have claimed to see her ghost wandering about the premises in a white nightgown.

Spreading out inland to the low foothills are the Pevensey Levels, tufted with sheep and sighing with reeds in its crackle-ware pattern of ditches. The best way to experience the real atmosphere of these breezy marshes, with their incessantly jubilant larks and the fidgety plop of unseen creatures below the dykes, is to take one of the tortuous lanes between high grasses, or a footpath such as the two-mile track towards Hooe. A heron will swoop, turn lazily and inquisitively above a ditch, and then settle like one of the splintered gateposts or unidentifiable stumps which jut up from abandoned paths and crumbling banks. A cricket scratches, lambs bleat and panic as an electric train rattles across the level towards Norman's Bay. To the north gleam the domes of the Royal Observatory. The steep pitched roofs of dolls'-house chalets along the seaward skyline look like a saw-toothed ridge of tank traps.

Pevensey is a Saxon village sheltering below a Roman castle wall which encloses a Norman keep. The walls of its church and many houses are as tough as the Roman bailey, their flints not decoratively knapped but rammed in whole. The Mint House contains a congested but entertaining gallimaufry of antiques, and there is a diminutive Court House.

Defenders of the castle had usually to be starved into submission, since direct assault on its massive bulk was so easily repelled. Bishop Odo of Bayeux held out against William Rufus for six weeks; in 1144 King Stephen's forces sat down outside until Matilda's men under the Earl of Clare succumbed to hunger; Simon de Montfort, failing to starve the occupants, had to give up his siege and go away. In 1399, while Sir John Pelham was away fighting in the cause of Henry Bolingbroke, his wife took personal charge of the castle's defence against Richard II's troops. In recognition of this and of the unwavering support of Sir John, the victorious Henry II awarded Pevensey to the Pelhams. Presented to the nation by the Duke of Devonshire, it is now in the care of the Department of the Environment. Appropriately enough, the first meeting of the Sussex Archaeological Society was held within the castle ruins soon after its formation in 1846.

The church has a Norman font. Its chancel dates from the time of King John, the main body of the present building a little later. A recent addition is a finely conceived steel angel,

designed by Leslie Benenson and made by Walter Woodward, which was installed in 1969. Below it hangs a corn dolly cross, like all corn dollies disturbingly pagan in spite of its Christian symbolism.

Disturbing in a different way is the experience of standing beneath the tower when the hour chimes. Each stroke sets up whispering, discordant resonances within the building and rattles the mechanism until one feels sure that something somewhere is bound to break loose and come tumbling down.

The road inland heads for Hailsham, but it is worth making a diversion into Polegate, on the main road out of Eastbourne, to visit its milling museum. This 85-foot tower mill was built in 1817 and was still in use just over 20 years ago. The museum is complete with the original applewood machinery.

Hailsham, to the north, is a market town of no special distinction but with little to its discredit. We are sure it would not have been locals who flouted the market facilities by rustling £500 worth of cattle and sheep from farms in the district, early in 1973.

Just outside the town to the west is Michelham Priory, an Augustinian house founded by Gilbert de Aquila of Pevensey in 1229 on an already moated site, fed by the Cuckmere. It was suppressed in 1536 and remained in private hands until 1959, when it was presented to the Sussex Archaeological Trust.

Between 1965 and 1969 the Conservation Corps did valiant work scouring out and deepening the choked moat, seven acres square. Centuries of neglect had silted it up so badly that there was a danger of its drying up altogether. Tons of reeds were shifted, and a reinforced concrete sluice introduced to check further silting.

The buildings, including a fourteenth-century three-storeyed gatehouse and a Tudor manor, have been restored and opened to the public, with period furnishings, a wheelwrights' museum, Sussex craft shop, and regular art exhibi-

18 *Petworth House*

tions in the great Tudor barn. On summer evenings there are performances of plays in the open air.

Near-by Dicker is associated with the black pottery known as Dicker ware, to be found in every local antique and souvenir shop.

To the east is another local speciality. The village of Herstmonceux is the centre of what may, accurately for once, be called a cottage industry. Its staple product is the Sussex trug, a shallow basket of wide, pliant strips of wood for carrying fruit and vegetables. Little workshops and stalls are to be found along the roadside from here through Windmill Hill towards Boreham Street.

Down a side road are the two establishments for which the place is best known: the castle, and the Royal Greenwich Observatory.

After the Norman Conquest the family of De Herst (from 'herst', 'hurst' or 'hyrst' meaning a wood) was linked by marriage with the De Monceux family, and so became Herst Monceux. Henry III spent a night in their manor house on his way to the battle of Lewes in 1264. In the fourteenth century it passed, again by marriage, to the Fynes or Fiennes. There is a splendid brass to Sir William Fiennes in the chancel of All Saints church, just outside the western gate of the grounds.

It is to Sir William's son Roger, one of the heroes of Agincourt, that we owe the present Herstmonceux Castle, one of the earliest and finest brick castles in the country. He brought Flemish craftsmen in to make and lay the bricks, with the intention of creating something warmer in appearance and more comfortable for habitation than the usual bleak stone fortress.

His son Richard married the heiress of the sixth Lord Dacre, and by patent duly became Lord Dacre of the South, to distinguish him from the Cumberland branch. The family continued to prosper, and seemed set for further advancement when Richard's great-great-grandson married the daughter of one of the most influential Sussex noblemen, the Earl of Abergavenny. Thomas, Lord Dacre, however, was a dissolute young scapegrace who revelled in the most unsuitable company and the most unsuitable diversions.

One day in April 1541 Thomas invited a dozen or so of his cronies to his home and 'there did legally conspire in what manner they could best hunt in the Park of Sir Nicholas Pelham . . . and bound themselves by oaths for such illegal purpose'. They reassembled ten days later and set out on their poaching expedition on Sir Nicholas's land. Three gamekeepers intercepted them near Hellingly, and in the hope of avoiding identification the intruders attacked, wounding one man so severely that he died within a couple of days. Tracked down, three of the party were accused of murder and hanged.

Lord Dacre had also been arrested. As a peer of the realm he had to be tried by a jury of his peers. At first he pleaded not guilty, on the grounds that he had not personally struck the fatal blow; but was persuaded to change his plea to one of guilty and ask for the king's mercy. Henry VIII was not a notably merciful man, and in any case could have been given little time in which to consider clemency: Thomas was hurried to his execution at Tyburn only two days after the trial ended.

The castle today, with its turrets, wide moat and tall gatehouse, is at first glance much as Sir Roger conceived it. It was by no means in this noble condition a couple of hundred years ago, when the roofs and much of the brickwork had crumbled. Large amounts of material were removed to build a new mansion at the northern end of the park. Partial restoration of the castle was carried out in 1910, and there were more substantial repairs by Sir Paul Latham in 1936.

In 1946 the Admiralty bought the property as a home for the Royal Greenwich Observatory, atmospheric pollution and the distortions of city lighting having made continuation of work near London well-nigh impossible. On 1 December

1967, just three centuries after Isaac Newton's invention of the world's first reflecting telescope, Queen Elizabeth II opened at Herstmonceux the new 89-inch telescope named in his honour. The dome in which it operates is open to the public all year round at the eastern entrance to the grounds, from which Halley Road leads to the castle and gardens and there joins a road named after Halley's predecessor, the first Astronomer Royal, Flamsteed. The gardens are open certain afternoons during the week, formal but luxuriant, with tantalising vistas between clipped, castellated hedges and artfully placed pillars and gateways.

In spite of its idyllic setting, all is not well with the Isaac Newton telescope. The choice of Herstmonceux as the site owed more, claim some astronomers, to chauvinism than to scientific appraisal. For the most protracted and fruitful use, it ought to have been established outside the British Isles, whose climatic conditions are unsatisfactory. The Sussex air may be clearer than most, but there is still a lot of cloud, and the telescope is operational for only about a third of the time available to large instruments in the Americas. Whether the whole thing will be transferred to a more suitable location is still a subject of debate. Alien as it may look in this rural setting, it would be missed if it now disappeared from the scene, especially as viewed from Pevensey Levels.

From Herstmonceux there is a choice of approaches to Bexhill. We can continue through Ninfield, close enough to the old iron furnaces to have had its stocks and whipping-post made of iron; or wind our way back across the levels to Pevensey and then out to Norman's Bay – now hedged with holiday homes – and Cooden Beach.

Cooden was once more heavily wooded than Ninfield is today. The forest came right down to the water's edge, and although that water has steadily pursued its own invasion and claimed much of the land for itself, blackened tree stumps can still be seen jutting from the sand and mud at low tide.

One of the last full-scale confrontations between smugglers and Preventive men took place just outside Bexhill on a night in 1828. The smugglers had unloaded the cargo and were on their way towards Sidley Green with a convoy of carts and pack-horses when a force of about 40 Preventive men caught up with them. A pitched battle was fought, in which an officer was killed and several others badly mauled. One elderly smuggler was shot and then vengefully mutilated by cutlasses, but kept such a firm hold on his club that next morning it was almost impossible to prise it loose. The Preventive or Blockade men were beaten off, but many of the smugglers had been recognised and were soon rounded up. Eight men were tried and sentenced to death, the sentence being eventually commuted to transportation.

The De La Warr Pavilion in Bexhill was one of the earliest multi-purpose entertainment complexes in the country and served as the model for many more; though, this being Bexhill, the entertainment has always been kept on a certain demure level. The town may not have Eastbourne's genteel pretensions, but it would never slip too perilously in the opposite direction – that direction being towards St Leonards and Hastings, almost joined up with it on its tatty eastern fringe.

Not that St Leonards itself would wish to be thought of as too brash a holiday centre. It has always rather fancied its relationship with Hastings as being similar to that of Hove with Brighton. It began as a separate town, its Georgian houses and hotels set along spacious thoroughfares, but as it spread into Warrior Square it found itself cheek by jowl with an imitative Hastings. In 1872 they were formally united under one borough corporation. An ornamental arch once spanned the promenade where they met, but has long since been superseded by a granite boundary stone.

The main stretch of entertainments, cafés, kiosks and

trinket shops really begins at the White Rock and extends to Rock-a-Nore in the east.

*   *   *

The name of White Rock might seem to indicate an outcrop of chalk hidden below the present bowling greens, model village, miniature golf course and gardens. But we left the chalkland at Eastbourne: the rock here is sandstone.

Until November 1834, when young Princess Victoria arrived for an extended holiday with her mother, there was in fact a heap of vast boulders on this spot, fragmented from the cliff behind. They accumulated until they formed a barrier across the shore and into the water. A road climbed over the hump, following the line of the hillside. The sea continued not only to pull down further rocks, often blocking the road, but to scour the edges of the little promontory itself, until its sides were bleached and polished and so stood out almost white against the darker background.

The Duchess of Kent had chosen to take her daughter, the future queen, to stay in St Leonards. Flooding, however, had made the always unreliable road from Hastings quite impassable, and on arrival the party and its welcoming dignitaries had to make a long detour. The immediate result was an indignant municipal decision to remove this obstacle. The boulders were broken up to form the basis of the present wide roadway and promenade, and the cliff behind was sheared off and strengthened by a retaining wall.

Today the White Rock Pavilion, an Italianate hall facing the pier, provides the usual variety shows and concerts. I associate it with matinées before the Second World War, when the Fol-de-Rols concert party came here season after season, and the Western Brothers strolled along the promenade before and after their performances, smiling amiably at their admirers. After the war there were concerts by the all-too-short-lived Southern Philharmonic Orchestra; and throughout the year there are still first-class concerts and recitals here. Alas, there are no longer the Western Brothers. Nor is there much left of the authentic old Hastings. Such as it is, it huddles below East Cliff, by its ruined harbour.

Hastings was a leading member of the Cinque Ports, the confederacy of key defence and supply points on the southeast coast whose first formal charter was granted by Edward I. The ports of Hastings, in Sussex, and Romney, Hythe, Dover and Sandwich in Kent, had formed an important alliance since the days of Edward the Confessor, and it has been plausibly suggested that this originated even earlier, being based on the Roman forts of the Saxon Shore. Sandwich replaced near-by Richborough, Dover remained as before, Hythe replaced Portus Lemanis (Lympne), Hastings covered the region once dominated by stranded Pevensey, while Romney filled in the marshy gap between Hythe and Hastings. To strengthen that exposed stretch still further, Rye and Winchelsea were added with full membership, though retaining their description of 'Ancient Townes' rather than making a new entity of Sept Ports. Later, each main port acquired subordinate 'limbs': Hastings, for example, was backed up by Pevensey and Seaford. All these towns were granted certain privileges in return for certain obligations.

Their first duty was to supply the Crown on demand with a specific number of ships for an agreed time, to give battle against the king's enemies or to transport troops to and from the Continent. In effect, throughout the Middle Ages the Cinque Ports provided the backbone of the royal fleet. Edward I used their ships for his Welsh and Scottish campaigns, and even before he got round to invading France they had inflicted a crushing defeat on a Norman fleet in a sort of privately arranged contest. A decline set in during the reign of Edward III, largely due to struggles with the unstable coastline, but even so a quarter of the English vessels at the victory of Sluys came from the Ports.

In 1474 Edward IV and his army were taken to and from France. In both 1513 and 1542 Henry VIII ordered the Cinque Ports navy to carry his men and horses to France. In answer to a command of Queen Elizabeth, the confederation 'set out five serviceable ships and a pinnace for Her Majesty's service for two months, but they served four months at their own costs'. As late as the reign of Charles I, when the region's naval resources had dwindled in comparison with those of the south-west coast and even of East Anglia, the Ports were still called on to put ships at the king's disposal for three months, 'which cost them £1,825 8s'.

Maintaining such vessels and putting them to sea at their own expense was a heavy burden. But the privileges offered in recompense were substantial. The Ports were free corporations, immune from feudal or shire obligations. They were exempt from panage, kaiage, murage, peisage, picage, terrage, scot and gild, hidage and scutage : that is, from taxes or tolls on pasturing hogs in forests, quay maintenance, town wall maintenance, use of a weigh-house, setting up a booth at a fair, anchorage in one of the king's harbours, personal activity and property, or on land or on exemption from military service. These concessions applied even outside their own local jurisdiction. A freeman of Rye reacted indignantly to an attempt to claim duty from him on corn bought in Hull, and after a stern rebuke from the Mayor and Jurats of Rye the Hull authorities meekly backed down.

Many administrative and ceremonial rights existed into our own time, including one exercisable at coronations, when 'the Barons of the Cinque Ports are wont, as of right they ought, to bear over the king and queen cloths of silk or gold, that is to say, by thirty-two Barons of the Cinque Ports; so, of right, that none other be amongst them to execute the said office'. The title of Baron did not bestow membership of the nobility, but signified only – and how dare I say 'only'? – that its holder was a freeman of the Ports. At the time of

Queen Elizabeth II's coronation one of the Sussex mayors summoned to attend was a sturdy, much loved local trades-man, who spent an unforgettable day in full regalia and then, less calculating and less quick off the mark than many of his own townspeople, found himself returning home on the last, late train in the luggage van, together with his robes in a cardboard box.

A Lord Warden of the Cinque Ports was appointed to guard the liberties and privileges of the confederation, mediating between Barons and Crown if disputes should arise. One of his perks of office was the right to all wrecks cast on shore between Seaford and Harwich. After the decline of the Ports, the position became more or less an honorary one. When the Duke of Wellington was petitioned by the townsfolk of Rye to speak up, in accordance with his oath of office, for their 'liberties, usages and customs' so that they might be declared freemen of their borough and be allowed to vote for their own member of Parliament, he made no attempt to endorse their or his own privileges. But then, the Iron Duke was notoriously in favour of gentlemen buying seats in Parlia-ment rather than demeaning themselves with the trivialities of elections; and, having himself been for a time M.P. for Rye, saw little reason to disturb procedures with which he had personally been in harmony.

In our own time the title has been bestowed as a mark of honour upon statesmen such as Sir Winston Churchill and Sir Robert Menzies.

In addition to their appearances before the Warden at what was known as the Court of Shepway, Barons and officials of the Ports ran their own local parliament, meeting when summoned at the Courts of Brotherhood and Guestling. Each full corporate member took it in turn to provide the Speaker for the Brotherhood, supported by two jurats and two com-moners. In addition, each member could send its own mayor, two jurats and two commoners, as guests, from which they were known as the Guestling. There is an obvious connection between such a gathering and the village of Guestling Green, on the road from Hastings to Winchelsea.

In spite of its early importance, Hastings was one of the first of the major ports to lose essential facilities. Its harbour persistently silted up, and in 1287 a terrible storm, which drowned old Winchelsea and crippled Romney, completed the ruin. Hastings struggled to retain its status and to re-fashion its harbour, but without success. The last effort at the end of the nineteenth century survives only as a ragged remnant of wall curving forlornly out into the waves. Even the smallest fishing boat has to be drawn up directly on to the Stade, the beach beside the tall, tarred huts in which nets are dried. These wooden skyscrapers were built high not merely for ease of hanging the nets, but because ground rents in Elizabethan times were also high, and it was more eco-nomic to extend vertically than horizontally.

If you stroll past the net shops, as they are known locally, on a Sunday evening in summer you may hear, above the traffic and the ubiquitous transistor radios, the sound of hymn-singing. It comes from the old fishermen's church, now used only for summer services, invariably ending with the supplication 'for those in peril on the sea'. At other times the little building serves as a fisherman's museum, squeezed around the *Enterprise*, the last purely sailing lugger built at Rock-a-Nore.

Behind the shore and the ice-cream parlours, what remains of the old town has been bisected by a broad main road along The Bourne. The bourne in question is a stream which still flows under the road and once supplied drinking water to the town, also serving unhygienically as a drain. Parallel with it on one side runs High Street, on the other All Saints Street, both lined with half-timbered houses, antique shops, tilting gables and façades of multi-coloured plaster. These were once neglected slums; now they are picturesque and fashionable. Behind High Street is pretty little Sinnock Square, as smart as a Chelsea mews, called after a butcher whose speciality had given it an earlier, sensibly discarded name: Tripe Alley. In All Saints Street is Shovells, a crouching little building which was once the home of the mother of Admiral Sir Cloudesley Shovell, hero of Barfleur and Gibraltar, who died with his entire crew when his ship went down off the Scillies.

All Saints church replaced an original destroyed during the disastrous year of 1377, when French pirates ravaged the whole coast, burning both Rottingdean and Rye. In that same year another Hastings church, St Clement's, was shattered. Completely rebuilt in 1390, it contains a souvenir of a further attack from the sea. In the seventeenth century a cannon-ball fired from a French or Dutch man-of-war embedded itself in the tower. Instead of gouging it out, the parishioners inserted another one close by to even up the pattern.

Remains of the church's original rood screen, long vanished, were discovered in 1933 incorporated in a neighbouring house, and brought back to their rightful setting. Near-by is a reproduction of the Bayeux Tapestry.

Dante Gabriel Rossetti and Elizabeth Siddall were married here on 23 May 1860, the bridegroom's name being for some reason registered as Daniel.

'Hastings hasn't a very large intelligentsia nowadays, has it?' This is another of those casually overheard remarks which one treasures, wondering what led up to it and how it will be resolved. I would not presume to speak for Hastings today, but on its past record it can hardly be said to have been shunned by the intelligentsia.

Rossetti first brought his favourite model, Elizabeth, here in 1854 in the hope of effecting some improvement in her health. They both found the town invigorating, and Elizabeth returned several times on her own. It was while she was staying here in 1860 that reports of her increasing illness brought Rossetti hurrying down to marry her.

Edward Lear enjoyed Hastings – 'where at least there are fresh air and muffins' – and persuaded Holman Hunt to stay here and paint. They both invited Millais to come and join them. Coventry Patmore lived for many years in Old Hastings House, still standing where High Street joins the main road, and instigated the building of the near-by Roman Catholic church of St Mary, Star of the Sea.

Rather less fond of the place, as one may deduce without any great literary acumen, was Robert Tressell, who pillories it as 'Mugsborough' in *The Ragged Trousered Philanthropists*.

Personally I prefer the picture of it as 'Marlingate', painted by Sheila Kaye-Smith. Apart from a few years in London after her marriage she never lived more than a few miles from her birthplace in Hastings, latterly at Northiam. The novels of her later years, unpretentious but observant and lucidly written, were all too easily dismissed as belonging in that indefinable category, 'women's fiction'. This does her memory a great disservice by blurring the true quality of her earlier, more vigorous books. Naïve and clumsy as it may be in parts, *The Tramping Methodist* was a remarkable book for an 18-year-old girl to write in the starchy provincial world of 1908, and it was followed by work of much greater force. There are resemblances to Thomas Hardy, but never a suggestion of a conscious echo: Sheila Kaye-Smith's moods and landscapes could only be those of Sussex, and her characters are firmly set in the county. Where there is melodrama, it is no more than the conventions of the time demanded; and real life, especially in the country, is often more melodramatic than a great many ascetic reviewers of fiction care to admit. I have not re-read *Sussex Gorse* for 20 years or so, but I well remember the feel of it. I say 'the feel of it' rather than its plot details or prose style: this is surely how we do recollect certain favourite books. Hastings itself is enshrined in

Tamarisk Town, the shrewd but affectionate story of the evolution of a seaside resort, with a few touches of Eastbourne just to confuse any pedantic, over-analytical reader.

To take in as wide a vista as possible of Hastings, a climb to the heights is essential. The least strenuous way is by funicular railway up East Hill, or by lift to West Hill, emerging below the green expanse of 'Ladies' Parlour', actually the old tilt-yard of the castle. The Conqueror's fortress is now in ruins, but still offers a dizzying panorama of the town it once dominated; and for those with a taste for the horrors, there are conducted tours around the still intact dungeons.

Some distance away is the entrance to other subterranean passages. The existence of St Clement's caves was well known before the beginning of the nineteenth century, above all to smugglers who gratefully made use of these extensive natural warehouses; but in 1812 the entrance was blocked up to exclude soldiers from the local garrison and various local ne'er-do-wells, who had been gambling and indulging in other immoralities within. Once sealed off, they were forgotten for some years until a householder working in his garden drove a pick through the rock and was tempted to explore further.

The sandstone must have been scoured away internally by prehistoric rivulets, and other fissures could have been formed by tremors after one of the great geological upheavals. There is no indication that Stone Age or other early men extended the caves or used them as the caves at such places as Altamira and Lascaux were used; but plenty of indication that later men made use of them.

Their re-discoverer set to work with one assistant to clean up the passages and make new ones. When he left the district the assistant, Joseph Golding, carried on the work with a will. He took a lease on the caves, carved out a new entrance and spacious new passage single-handed, and by candle-light carved a number of statues from the solid rock. Today they are lit by electricity, and the largest cave is used as a ballroom, with a bar kept well stocked by citizens more law-abiding than the smugglers who might once have offered cut-price terms from their neighbouring vaults.

From East Hill, paths lead into the bucolic cleft of Ecclesbourne Glen and on to Fairlight and the Fire Hills, ablaze with gorse like some sprawling yellow-beamed lighthouse above the sea.

The gnarled crag soars to almost 500 feet before the aspiring finger of Fairlight church tower, visible for miles from sea and land. Lovers' Seat has had to be moved back from the unstable edge, but still attracts its quota of romantic visitors.

At the end of the eighteenth century, when there were no trippers and the village had not even begun to spread down towards the cove, this was a suitably lonely rendezvous for a young couple avoiding the vigilance of disapproving parents. Captain Lamb of Rye, in command of a revenue cutter, had fallen in love with a Miss Boys from Hawkhurst. Her mother and father, considering him an unworthy match, sent the girl for a holiday to remote Fairlight Place, in the hope that she would forget him and that in any case he would not be able to make contact with her. They must have been a rather slow-witted couple to have chosen a spot so close to the Channel, the young officer's normal highway. Contact was speedily established, and when the coast was clear the amorous Miss Boys would signal to her beloved in the bay below. He must have had a better head for heights than I have, since he at once climbed up the cliff to meet her.

There are many versions of the story including the inevitable one with a tragic ending, consigning both of them to a watery grave. In real life, it was only Lamb who drowned, and that not until many years later. He and his lady were married at St Clement Danes in London and settled at Salehurst, where they lived happily for nigh on 30 years until the husband died in a yachting accident.

Behind this headland lie Pett and the plunge to the levels, different in every respect from what we have just seen. Cliff End is indeed the end of one world and the beginning of another. I am proposing not to cross the boundary at this moment, but to leave exploration of that region until the right time, the logical place: the end of the book, the end of the county.

So back we turn towards Eastbourne and the chalk uplands.

The South Downs

'The wide-sweeping Downs are pressed upon by the plough on the one side and by Building Societies on the other'. It sounds a very contemporary plaint. In fact it was the opinion of a contributor to the *Brighton Herald* nigh on a hundred years ago.

In 1973 a writer to *The Times* grieved that wild flowers, and in particular wild thyme, were vanishing from the Downs because of the depredations of ploughs and rotary cutters, and the substitution of beef cattle for sheep. Even the ramparts and interiors of the ancient hill forts, protected from modern farming methods, are denuded by ramblers who pick the flowers and gradually kill off the strain.

All change is suspect, especially to those who have known and loved a region for years, perhaps since childhood. In my own lifetime the Downs have altered considerably; yet taken all in all, far less so than the coast and the towns and villages whose fate it has been to be linked by busy roads and to sprout housing estates and light industrial complexes. Kipling's 'blunt, bowheaded, whalebacked Downs' are not so bare as they used to be, but they are no less noble. The downland shepherd with his crook is no longer the archetypal figure. The drovers who knew every lane and ridgeway, every watering place for the travelling flock, and every skill in controlling great numbers of beasts to avoid loss or injury, are no longer the aristocrats of their society. Still the sheep population is a significant one; and the invading cornfields, so far from distorting the whalebacks, add new textures, rippling and amber under the breeze, darkening with stubble, changing with the seasons and changing under sun and cloud. At times one almost believes in the existence, somewhere far

behind and far above, of a bulbous-cheeked wind god puffing frivolously, as from the corner of some old map, so that as far as the eye can see a broad wave of grass or golden grain bows under his breath, contained between banks of more placid green and gold. The crests of the hills pulse and breathe. A vast, lazy yet restless creature stretches itself then subsides, relaxing under the stroking and ruffling of hairs along its flank.

There is really only one way to experience both the strength and the gentleness of this creature, and that is to walk along its back.

On St Swithin's Day in 1972 Lord Shawcross formally declared open the South Downs Way, 80 miles of footpath and bridleway for public use from Beachy Head to the Hampshire border. Already there is approval in principle for its continuance to Winchester and eventually, it is hoped, to Salisbury.

The official establishment of this right of way is the fulfilment of what might be called a walker's or rider's dream were it not that it has been achieved by years of hard work, hard argument, and precious little dreaming.

After the Second World War more than half the footpaths in the county, on the Downs and in the woodlands of the Weald, had been obscured. Some had been choked by unfettered undergrowth; some were obliterated under the farmlands of those who had quite rightly dug and sown for victory; some patches had to be cleared of bombs and unexploded shells. While no farmer would knowingly leave high explosives on his land as a deterrent to trespassers, there is little doubt that many would have been only too glad to let rights of way be neglected and ultimately forgotten. Fortunately there were vigilant local patriots who, having answered the call to protect all that was best in England from its foreign enemies and carried out their duties in that cause, continued to protect their cherished land from its would-be

20 *The Causeway, Horsham*

exploiters. Ancient rights must not be lost by default. Despite legislation, including an enlightened Act of 1968, to clarify the responsibilities of county councils, parish authorities and landowners, there was and is a lot of official apathy or evasiveness to be combated.

The Society of Sussex Downsmen, the Sussex Rights of Way Group and other amenity groups keep a watchful eye not just on large-scale bureaucratic or commercial threats to their communities but on the slightest infringement of rights to their footpaths, bridleways and open spaces. Often they are compelled to take on work in clearing obstructions which should be local or county council responsibility. When they find notices defaced, decrepit or mysteriously removed, they take action. It can be a frustrating business, most of all when they find they are having to challenge the very authorities who ought to be working on their behalf. All too often the feeling grows that officialdom is at best careless, at worst actively against the individual or small group.

'The interpretation of public notices is often difficult at the best of times', lamented a recent report, 'but when, as often happens, they are planted in the wrong places, the whole thing becomes quite uncomprehensible. Quite unnecessary anxiety, confusion and formal objections result . . . it all adds to cost and delay in securing usable paths'.

A typical experience is that of a West Sussex man who recommended to his son a delightful walk from Arundel to Burpham, only to find that a small typewritten notice had been affixed in a corner where it was unlikely to attract any attention, announcing the closure of the footpath, giving no reasons, and stating simply that all objections must be lodged within six weeks. Even when people are alerted in time, such objections are all too often ignored unless backed by voluble pressure groups, and at best bland assurances are given that alternative tracks will be provided – routes which, as the objectors learn too late, will not have the same legal protection as those about to be extinguished and so will be liable to extinction themselves whenever it suits the local authority. Even with genuine co-operation from local authorities there are innumerable minor issues which cannot all be dealt with at once yet which, if not dealt with, can mean the loss or undesirable temporary abandonment of some valuable asset to the life of the community. The most energetic county council has no way of knowing when some remote signpost has fallen down; and, when informed, cannot rush a man immediately to the spot. Much depends on groups and individuals fond enough of their environment to do something about it.

The cost of replacing or installing new metal signposts is prohibitive, says an official. Use wooden ones, says the Rights of Way Group : more in keeping with the surroundings, and a lot cheaper. But there is a danger of the lettering being obscured or impregnated with moss. Then volunteers will keep an eye open for such deterioration, and clean them out.

Volunteers clean out quite a lot of things. It was not enough to strive for clearance of overgrown footpaths and open spaces after the war : left to themselves, they will soon be reconquered. Where some folk spend part of the week-end washing or tinkering with their cars, others are plunging into miniature jungles of creepers and nettles. 'Incredible what half a dozen really determined people can do in three or four hours on a Sunday afternoon', observes Charles Shippam of Boxgrove, himself a pretty energetic supporter of the Rights of Way Group and of the Downsmen. But as we talked he added ruefully : 'We don't get so many of the younger people nowadays. Canals and archaeology are more romantic than tugging away at undergrowth and tidying paths'.

He and his unflagging colleagues have been gratified to find that the opinion of even the most recalcitrant farmers is swinging round in support of their aims and methods, and for a long time now they have been on the best of terms with keepers, foresters, agents and farm managers on the larger estates, who recognise the genuine enthusiasts and usually collaborate willingly.

Charles Shippam also keeps up to date a useful list of accommodation and refreshment places near to key points along the South Downs Way, complete with details of grazing and stabling for mounts. Copies are available from the Countryside Commission, who issue a leaflet containing a map and advice on various aspects of the route.

The trackway begins above Eastbourne and makes its way along ridges and down through the river valleys, taking in villages such as Alfriston, Southease and Amberley, then escaping again to the airy heights of Ditchling Beacon, Chanctonbury, and Beacon Hill. Much of it follows the course trodden by Stone Age and Bronze Age men, and later by the Celts. It was not merely a trade route but a pilgrims' way to distant Avebury and Stonehenge. Modern oak signposts and stone markers now define the path, undeclamatory but unmistakable with their stylised symbol of an acorn. Cyclists, as well as pedestrians and equestrians, are allowed along most stretches; but I fancy it must be a bumpy ride, and one calling for frequent investment in new tyres.

After an hour or so on a sunny day the traveller may begin to think longingly of cool drinks. This is the signal for a descent to one of the villages tucked away in some small coombe, or nestling at the very foot of the hills. There are few settlements at all high on the Downs, other than little Telscombe. Neolithic man and his immediate successors must either have had some of the properties of the camel or the natural water resources on the heights must have been better in his day than in ours. It does seem likely that up to about 2500 B.C. the Downs were lightly wooded with oak, and the climate was fairly wet. With the coming of drier conditions, the trees were enfeebled, and also suffered clearances when the Beaker Folk began cultivation. Perhaps these folk or their children lived to regret this destruction, just as Norfolk farmers are beginning to doubt the wisdom of having uprooted so many hedges in the cause of supposedly easier large-scale agriculture.

From Eastbourne there are, at the start, alternative routes which unite at Alfriston. One follows the cliffs along the rim of the Seven Sisters Country Park – definitely not for cyclists or those on horseback; the other over Willingdon Hill goes through Jevington, an attractive hamlet on an attractive road between Polegate and Eastdean.

The relics of Eastdean's past create a tougher impression than its picturesque present. The church tower has walls three feet thick. The sturdy, now smart little houses were once the homes of wreckers and smugglers, and the local inn was one of their best-known meeting places. An imposing fireback in the bar, dated 1622, came here from near-by Friston Place. At one time a tax of a penny had to be paid each time the fire was lit. The inn is respectfully named after the animal on the lord of the manor's escutcheon. At least that was the idea : it was not until after the place had become well established as the *Tiger* that it was realised the beast on the coat of arms was in fact a leopard.

Tucked away in the woods beyond Friston is Westdean, with a well-restored parsonage house and many memories of Alfred the Great. When the River Cuckmere was a broader and deeper estuary than it is now, he kept a fleet here, and built a palace where Bishop Asser, his biographer, is thought to have met him for the first time.

Charleston Manor is a harmonious blend of Norman, Tudor and early Georgian elements. It has spacious gardens and one of the mightiest tithe barns in the land. The Norman wing was for a time the home of William I's cup-bearer.

Confusingly, there are an East Dean and West Dean farther along the Downs, in West Sussex. I note that in recent years the eastern pair tend to have their names printed on maps and official documents as one word, to distinguish them from their distant cousins.

Approaching Alfriston, the driver turning in from the A.27 is treated to a better perspective than the walker on Windover Hill. Using the Wilmington by-road, he has both the priory and the tallest man in the kingdom to contemplate. Robert de Mortain, William I's half-brother, was awarded the Rape of Pevensey, and as a pious gesture allocated the manor of Wilmington to Grestain Abbey in Normandy. A small priory founded here became headquarters for administration of estates held in other countries. During the Hundred Years War it was dissolved on the grounds of this undesirable French connection, and in due course became a manor house and farm. It is now cared for by the Sussex Archaeological Trust. One wonders how the monks reacted to the perpetual blank stare of the 240-foot pagan Long Man, for ever leaning on his staves. One account has it that the original figure had a sexual endowment such as the Cerne Abbas giant's, which the monks austerely etched out. Another denies that the figure was even here at the time, and ascribes it to a scholarly prank not so many centuries old. Rather an arduous prank, considering the labour involved.

Wilmington's little church contains a Jacobean canopied pulpit, and its churchyard an outsize yew claiming to be the oldest in the county, perhaps older than the church itself.

Uphill are Lullington and Litlington: uphill, then plungingly downhill, the road clinging to the side of the Down and then sliding thankfully towards the tranquillity of the Cuckmere valley. Of Lullington's Norman church only the chancel, 16 feet square, remains, capped by a shingled bell-cote. Litlington is pretty but often somewhat overcrowded for what little it has to offer, having doubtless attracted an overspill of visitors from its more impressive neighbour.

Alfriston is beautifully set in the meadows of the Cuckmere. Its large fourteenth-century cruciform church comes as a shock after the smaller, cosier ones we have so recently passed, and merits its description as 'cathedral of the Downs'. The marriage register goes back to 1504 and could be the oldest in England.

Close to one corner of the churchyard is the Old Clergy House, a rare survival of a pre-Reformation priest's abode, with fine roof timbers and posts in its simple living-room. For generations it was used as a cottage, until declared unfit for further occupation. In 1896 it became the first building to be purchased by the National Trust, formed only the year before.

A long way back, earlier than church or clergy house, there was an extensive Saxon cemetery in this valley. It was exposed again when foundations for a house were being dug, revealing great numbers of broken skeletons, among them that of a crippled but obviously wealthy woman surrounded by her personal treasures. Items removed to the Sussex Archaeological Society's museum in Lewes include amber and porcelain beads, bronze ornaments, iron weapons, and even some little-damaged glass.

Alfriston, being by nature so attractive, now attracts more visitors than it can comfortably cope with. The famous *Star Inn*, busily expanding to the rear, seems in danger of becoming a motel; but it still presents its same appealing face to the street, and its red wooden lion figurehead still grins widely on its corner. This figure is thought to have come from a seventeenth-century wreck on the coast a few miles away. We can only hope the wreck was not deliberately engineered: Alfriston men were as busy as any of their neighbours when it came to wrecking and smuggling, making good use of the winding Cuckmere to ship goods up into the village. The *Star* is reputed to have a subterranean passage to the seashore. but digging such a passage through the largely marshy surroundings would surely have been too formidable a labour for its possible returns: the river was swifter and simpler.

Another smugglers' centre was *Market Cross House*. The market cross itself has stood beside it since the fifteenth century – or did so until 1955, when a lorry blundered into it and brought it down. The present cross was reconstructed from old stones similar to those in the original.

The road out towards Berwick takes us past Drusilla's. To be precise, it will take us past provided we have no children with us. The zoo and gardens have been there for half a century now, and have lost none of their appeal. Captain Ann bought the property in 1923, began serving teas in the cottage, and soon added a miniature railway and pets' corners. Today his family carry on the business and have introduced an aquarium, aviaries, a penguin pool, and a farm playground.

Contemporary additions have been made, too, to Berwick church. The screen, pulpit and other parts of the interior were gaily painted by Quentin and Vanessa Bell and Duncan Grant when they lived near by.

Walkers and motorists can both take advantage of a favourite picnic spot, High and Over (frequently condensed to Hindover), off the road between Alfriston and Seaford, with wide-ranging views over sea and river valley. The driver may then be in danger, though, of descending into Seaford. The persevering walker should head for the next of the great vantage points, Firle Beacon, which at over 700 feet is the highest point in this eastern part. Below and around it are barrows and tumuli, patterns of Celtic fields, and a number of lesser but jaunty eminences. The church at West Firle has brasses and monuments to the Gage family, whose Suffolk branch introduced the greengage into this country.

The South Downs Way crosses the river Ouse near Southease, but there is another route down through Glynde, crossing the tributary Glynde Reach.

Glynde Place was once the home of Colonel Herbert Morley, a member of Parliament for Lewes and, during the Commonwealth, for Rye. Of the 59 commissioners who signed Charles I's death warrant, seven were Sussex men. Colonel Morley provided a regiment for Parliament from his own friends, tenants and constituents, defended Lewes against a Royalist attack, and remained true to the Parliamentary cause; but could not bring himself to approve of the king's execution, and for much of the Protectorate remained secluded in Glynde. Having helped Waller to recapture Arundel, he was, as we have mentioned, appointed joint governor of the castle with young William Springet, and it was in fact Morley into whom Charles II nearly bumped during his escape. It's difficult not to speculate whether the colonel, who must have known the tall, dark-featured young man well by sight, in fact recognised him but was unwilling to turn him over to doubtful justice.

In 1659 Morley was appointed lieutenant of the Tower of London, and was urged by friends, including the diarist John Evelyn, to set in motion the procedure of recalling King Charles II. Although he foresaw this move as inevitable, Morley did not wish to ingratiate himself with the exiled king by putting his old comrades-in-arms in jeopardy. It was left to General Monk to effect the Restoration.

After Charles's return, many who had been specifically excluded from the proposed Bill of Indemnity had to flee abroad, some of them being shipped out at night in circumstances ironically like those which Charles himself had once experienced. Morley escaped such retribution. He yielded up the Tower and formally sought the king's pardon. It was granted for a fee of £1,000. One or two accounts say that Morley again retired to Glynde, this time for good, and ended his days there in obscurity. This is not so. The king's brother, James, Duke of York, was appointed Lord Warden of the Cinque Ports in 1660, and in 1661 exercised his prerogative of recommending a member of Parliament to the electors of Rye. He forced on them a man of whom they had never heard; but when it came to the second member, they chose

Colonel Herbert Morley, who had served them before and whom they all respected. Morley continued to serve until his death in 1667.

In 1901 Frances, daughter of the first Viscount Wolseley, who as Sir Garnet Wolseley had been a national hero and added a catch-phrase to the English language, founded the College of Lady Gardeners at Glynde. She laid out gardens at 'Ragged Lands', Glynde, and in 1917 started a school at Scaynes Hill to train women in the management of small-holdings. Anxious to assemble an authoritative collection of her distinguished father's papers, she was unfortunately in-volved in a dispute with her mother, who wilfully scattered family belongings and documents among several different institutions. In the end the main body of the material was pulled together again and lodged in what is now the Wolseley Room of Hove Central Library, along with a collection of other material on Sussex subjects.

A mile from the village is a place better know than Glynde itself. More than a quarter of a century before West Sussex staged its Chichester Festival, there was a Glyndebourne Festival. John Christie, owner of the estate, had married the operatic soprano Audrey Mildmay, and between them they decided to add an opera house to their home. Its first season began in May 1934, when afternoon travellers through Victoria station were taken aback to see a small group of men and women in evening dress boarding a special train. The following day another group followed in their footsteps: seven people, to be exact. Later bookings were rather heal-thier, though for many years the festival made a sizeable loss.

With Carl Ebert as artistic director and Fritz Busch as con-ductor, the opening production of *Le Nozze di Figaro* set the tone for subsequent seasons. Christie had originally favoured a Wagnerian repertoire, but his wife urged that they should concentrate on Mozart, which, with only a couple of diversions, they did until after the Second World War. Since then there have been several experiments: the rediscovery of Monteverdi's dramatic genius and the encouragement of some younger contemporary composers have been due in no small measure to Glyndebourne's policy.

What makes people dress up in the middle of what may well be a hot afternoon and make the journey to rural Sussex? First of all, of course, the quality of the performances; a *soupçon* of snobbery, undoubtedly: but also a sense of occasion. Television, they say, has killed the cinema. It is too much trouble to go round the corner. Radio gramophone records and tapes might be supposed to have the same effect on concerts, ballet and opera. Strangely, concert halls and opera houses have never been better attended. There is something in the mere fact of making the effort which adds to the ultimate pleasure, whether that effort takes one to Chichester, Aldeburgh, or Glyndebourne.

Audrey Mildmay not only took an energetic part in the planning of all performances, and sang in many of them, but after the war had a lot to do with the establishment of the Edinburgh Festival. She died just before the coronation of Queen Elizabeth ii.

Between Glynde and Lewes rears the shoulder of Mount Caburn. It is by no means as lofty as Firle Beacon or the intervening Beddingham Hill, but it commands just as exhilarating a landscape. Surveying the world from here, it is impossible not to sympathise with the local farmer who shuddered at the mere idea of visiting London: 'They don't get any air up there till we've finished with it'.

*　　*　　*

Entering Lewes from below Malling Hill and the golf course, the road passes a public house called the *Snowdrop*. Its name commemorates not the delicate spring flower but something far less delightful.

Just before Christmas 1836 the wind blew swirling snow-storms across the country. By Christmas Night roads and lanes around Lewes were blocked, and the only way in or out of the town was by river. A group of cottages known as Boulder Row stood along the Malling road, overshadowed by the looming cliff behind, which had been increased by a 15-foot snowdrift piled on top. Some cottagers were persuaded to leave, but others remained stubborn and so were killed when at last the snow wall cracked and came down in an avalanche, smashing the cottages and hurling débris far across the road. More snow fell as rescuers tried to dig the victims out.

Lewes itself is a steep town. Its name derives, with good reason, from the Old English *hlaew*, meaning a hill. Few driving experiences are more disquieting than to be on School Hill behind a laden car transporter which has stopped on the entry to High Street. The town grew downwards from its castle, established above the River Ouse by the Norman baron of the Rape of Lewes, William de Warenne. His original Norman gatehouse has been almost swallowed up by the projecting fourteenth-century barbican built into the moat and reinforced by sentinel towers on either side, one of which has been beheaded. There is some good flintwork here and in near-by walls. Inside, the castle has not one motte but two: the nearer, more imposing mound supports the keep, while Black Mount to the north commands the valley of the Ouse. The keep was supplemented in the thirteenth century by four towers, two of which remain. In the heart of it all is the setting for a game which has been popular throughout the castle's history – a bowling green.

In the lane leading to the gatehouse is a sixteenth-century building refaced in Georgian brickwork which contains one of the museums administered by the Sussex Archaeological Society. Their collections were originally housed in the castle keep, but are now well displayed in Barbican House. There are specimens of Wealden iron, including some magnificent firebacks, and coins struck at various Sussex mints, Sussex pottery, drawings and tapestries, and models of ancient villages. Another museum, devoted to folklore, is in the suberb of Southover at Anne of Cleves House, one of the residences given by Henry VIII to his hastily discarded (though for once not decapitated) wife.

Also in Southover are the remains of the once massive Priory of St Pancras. De Warenne and his wife Gundrada, at one time thought to have been the Conqueror's daughter, built here in 1077 a stone church which they presented to monks of the Cluniac order in place of an earlier Saxon timber building. The mother house at Cluny was one of the most powerful monasteries in Europe, and the priory which grew up at Southover soon became its cherished senior daughter in England. De Warenne authorised its collection of tithes and its freedom of pasture and fishing rights, and in a charter granted to the monks

preferential buying of logs for making their
wood pile on three days of the week . . . from
Whitsun to Lammas, and after the said feast
common market with the men of Lewes if
necessary. And of all flesh and fish and
all other things which they wish and require
to buy for their own needs or those of their
guests, not only in the vill of Lewes but
also at Seaford and throughout my estates in
all places where a market is held, I grant
to the monks for ever that every day they
may have without hindrance of impediment the
pre-emption after sufficient purchases have
been made for my own needs and those of my
heirs.

The family continued its patronage of the priory, and other devout neighbours added their contributions. In its turn the priory leased out many of the lands and concessions donated, drawing substantial rents or stipulating in lieu services such as ploughing, sowing, reaping and carting, or the provision of certain foods at certain times of year.

In May 1264 the priory was taken over as headquarters by Henry III, preparing for battle with Simon de Montfort in the Barons' War. De Montfort, reconnoitring from his camp at Fletching, planned a surprise advance along an old sunken trackway, and on 14 May met the royal troops below Mount Harry, near the present racecourse. The king had twice as many men as the earl, including a cavalry force under his son Prince Edward, later to be King Edward I. The first cavalry charge scattered the barons' foot soldiers, but in pursuing them, and in being diverted for some reason never satisfactorily explained to a near-by hilltop, Edward's horsemen lost their advantage. By the time they regrouped and returned to the scene of the main conflict it was too late to save the day.

Henry was defeated, and in the priory signed the treaty known as the Mise of Lewes, by which Edward was held hostage as guarantee of his father's good conduct, and which led in due course to de Montfort's calling a representative assembly on which the later development of our House of Commons was based.

Hundreds of skeletons from the battle have been found at one time and another near the site of the present gaol, and in the Offham chalkpits.

At the Reformation the priory suffered its final humiliation. It was among the properties granted to Thomas Cromwell in gratitude for his labours on the king's behalf against the monasteries. Cromwell showed his continuing sincerity in this cause by engaging an Italian engineer to demolish the St Pancras buildings as thoroughly as possible.

The fabric of the great religious houses had been effectively destroyed by Henry VIII, but when his daughter Mary came to the throne she was determined to restore at least the spirit of the Roman church. Where her father and his henchmen had desecrated and burned buildings, she set about burning human flesh. Between 1555 and 1557 17 men and women, from a Sussex total of 33, were burned at the stake in Lewes High Street. One of them, Thomas Read, apparently had some last-minute doubts and decided, the night before his arrest, that he would go to church and accept its rituals. But then he had a vision of 'a company of tall young men in white, very pleasant to behold, to whom he would have joined himself; but it would not be. Then he looked on himself and he was full of spots, and therewith waked, and took hold and stood to the truth'. In 1901 an obelisk was set up on Cliffe Hill in memory of the martyrs.

Perhaps it is this lingering memory which accounts for the vigour with which Bonfire Night is still celebrated here, and why the custom of burning the Pope in effigy persisted when most communities were content with the less provocative, though equally incendiary, Guy.

The western slopes of the Ouse valley sprout a number of agreeable little villages, edging coyly back from the road to Newhaven. Kingston-near-Lewes is in danger of becoming Kingston-within-Lewes, but so far has managed to retain its individuality and its sure escape route to the Downs. Its church is dedicated to St Pancras, patron saint of the lost priory. Iford church has a central tower dividing nave from transept; Southease and Piddinghoe both have round towers, probably useful as beacons to ships on their way upstream to Lewes. Rodmell church has a huge font of Sussex marble, and in the churchyard a substantial gravestone in the shape of a millstone, marking the grave of Rodmell's last miller.

The village is little more than one flinty street like a strung-out line of farm buildings converted into cottages, their trim gardens enclosed by the sternest of flint walls. The letter 'A' appearing on many houses, and the name of the local pub, recall the days up to the end of the First World War when the entire estate belonged to the Marquis of Abergavenny.

Monks House was for a long time thought to have been a house of retreat attached to the priory of St Pancras. When they bought it in 1919, Leonard and Virginia Woolf fondly encouraged themselves to believe this, but later Woolf found it to be untrue. From 1707 until the time they took it over, it had been in the occupation of only three families. In the fourth volume of his autobiography Leonard Woolf describes the sadness of the summer's day when he watched the auction of personal effects of the deceased Verralls from whose heirs he had bought the house.

In spite of that inevitably melancholy spectacle, Monks House itself provided the Woolfs with many consolations. It had the atmosphere of a happily lived-in house, and on more than one occasion Virginia Woolf hurried thankfully back to it when threatened by one of her recurrent nervous depressions. Congenial friends such as T. S. Eliot, Maynard Keynes and Kingsley Martin came to visit and to argue. Less congenially, the wireless brought threats to their peace and that of their friends. On the last page of *Downhill all the Way*, Leonard Woolf recalls one day in 1939 when he was planting iris reticulata in the orchard, and his wife called to him that a speech by Hitler was being broadcast. He refused to go indoors. 'I'm planting iris, and they will be flowering long after he is dead'. Hitler's war precipitated Virginia Woolf's decline and eventual suicide; but in 1966 her widower was able to record that, 21 years after Hitler's death, some of those flowers still thrived.

Other growths have flourished here. In the time of James I some of the earliest mulberry trees in the country were planted here. For some years the village had a profitable little silk industry.

21 *Sackvilles in the Buckhurst Chapel, Withyham Church*

Rodmell sits with some complacency between the comfortable-sounding Southease and Northease. This latter hamlet sports a mysterious dewpond which may have existed since the Stone Age. Dewponds are a familiar but often puzzling phenomenon upon the Downs. Their saucer-shaped depressions, often reinforced in our own times with concrete, are known to fill when there has been no rain, and it has therefore been assumed that the beneficent spirits of evening and morning have replenished them with dew. It depends what one means by dew. In most cases the deposits are probably due to condensation of heavy mist. But, as the people of Northease will point out, their pond is often nicely supplied when there has been no such mist. Apparently some localised freak of temperature or pressure change, or both, produces an unusual condensation here.

From Southease a road strikes uphill from the main highway, coming to an end in Telscombe, which has so little in common with the hutches of Telscombe Cliffs that it does not countenance more than a rough track between them. The village church has been over-restored, but otherwise the little enclave is unspoilt. It has every intention of remaining so. The manor house and gardens, with some neighbouring land, are under the charge of the National Trust, though not open to the public. The village as a whole has bequeathed itself to Brighton and is administered by six corporation trustees, to ensure that it shall never be tarnished.

It was on the tracts of downland around here that a young shepherd found time to think and study. John Dudeney was born in 1782, the son of a Rottingdean shepherd, and spent some of his childhood at Plumpton with his grandfather. From the age of eight onwards he helped to look after the sheep. Everyone, even the youngest child, had to do what he could for the family. 'I had a good father and mother', Dudeney recalled later, 'though they were poor, my father's wages being only £30 a year, and the keeping of ten or twelve

22 *Ashdown Forest*

sheep, having a family of ten children, yet we were never in want'. Like others in that lonely occupation, he caught wheat-ears to supplement his meagre diet and meagre income, selling them and plovers' eggs in the coastal towns and villages. John Dudeney was anxious to increase his income not merely out of sheer material necessity, but to satisfy his ruling passion. When he was ten a visitor had given him a history book and a copy of *Robinson Crusoe*, and from then on his hunger for books and knowledge was insatiable. 'When I came to the fairs, I brought all the money I could spare to buy books'. Taken on as under-shepherd by a farmer near Kingston, he was delighted to receive the higher wage of £6 a year. By catching wheatears and, during the winter, moles, he found he could spare a little more money. In the coldest of weathers he would pace up and down to keep himself warm, reading all the time. At the age of 20 he began to teach himself geometry. Digging a hole in the hillside, he kept books, a slate, and a pair of iron compasses within, covered by a large flint.

Three years later he gave up the solitary life and found himself another flock. Having taught himself so much, he now set about teaching others, and became a schoolmaster in Lewes, where he died in 1852. Testimonies to his qualities and the affection in which he was held would indicate that the patience acquired on the lonely hills stood him and his pupils in good stead. The rhythm of the sheepman's year must have established a rhythm in a man's own blood. Bob Copper in his richly reminiscent, heartwarming book, *A Song for Every Season*, sums it up admirably when he describes an uncle whose 'actions, speech and thought were all geared down in speed and proclaimed an inner peace that made his presence as soothing and reassuring as the slow, quiet ticking of a grandfather clock'.

John Dudeney could not resist going back from time to time to see whether his cache still existed, and for 30 years was able to identify it, 'and I have several times gone a little way out of my road to visit it and offer up my thanks to that gracious Providence who has so directed my way'. He was sad when, at last, it was ploughed over and he could no longer find the exact spot.

Plumpton had previously accommodated another, very different scholar: one with more leisure and more ample means with which to indulge his tastes. Leonard Mascall, who lived at moated Plumpton Place during the time of Henry VIII and the reigns of Henry's three successors, wrote some of the first countryside and 'popular gardening' books in English. The title of the first, actually a translation, would perhaps not be too favourably received by a modern publisher worried about the jacket layout and the positioning of the spine lettering: *A Book of the Arte and Manner how to Graft and Plante all Sortes of Trees, how to set Stones and Sow Pepins*. He is credited with having introduced the golden pippin into this country, and in the same year introduced golden carp into his moat.

His moat is now dry, Plumpton Place now an agricultural college. In general the district is associated in most people's minds with the steeplechase course.

On a hillside south of the village a V-shaped plantation of firs commemorates Queen Victoria's Golden Jubilee. There was once a cross cut into the chalk, also visible from many local vantage points, supposedly marking the burial-place of many slain in the battle of Lewes, but nobody has troubled to maintain it, and if any trace still exists it must be detectable only in an aerial photograph.

Another commanding height on the route of the South Downs Way is Ditchling Beacon, used quite literally as a beacon in the chain of fires kindled to announce the coming of the Spanish Armada. Ditchling itself is one of the most alluring of the villages which, set a little way back from the

Downs, belong irrevocably to the Downs. Its timbered frontages, its red roofs and its spacious surrounding fields and commons, undulating like the last breaking ripples of the high waves in the south, have attracted many writers and painters to work here and settle here. Esther Meynell has written most lyrically of it. Sir Frank Brangwyn painted here, and died here in 1956. Among its grander buildings is the house of Anne of Cleves, with its private chapel and walled garden, another of the bribes offered to her by Henry VIII. There is little evidence that she spent any time here: but then, it would have been quite a task for her to ration out her presence fairly among all the desirable properties she had acquired.

Visible from the Beacon, and from many other angles, are Jack and Jill. These two windmills, black tower and white post, have stood side by side for many years, established in defiance of the old fear that the more windmills you had in any one region, the less air they'd have between them. (My uncle knows of a contradictory version which claims the reason for recent blustery winters as being that too many mills have been abandoned, and so don't use up the wind the way they used to). Jill, the white lady, was built 150 years ago at Patcham, now almost swallowed up by Brighton. She was later shifted bodily to Clayton, and in 1876 Jack was built to keep her company. Jill worked until 1909, Jack went on for a further 20 years. Struck by lightning, he lost his sails, and spent many more years as a sad, gaunt pillar beside his more graceful girl friend. In 1973 a film company came to the rescue. Needing two such windmills to play important though non-speaking roles in a film thriller, they engaged two local millwrights to fit Jack with new sails. The job cost about £3,000, and although Jack is still not restored to full working order he looks a lot better for the face-lift.

Near Patcham, Jill's birthplace, is a marble temple, startling and exotic in this setting. It is the Chattri memorial, dedicated in 1921 by the Prince of Wales (later, briefly, Edward VIII) to

Indian soldiers who had died for the Allied cause in the First World War.

For generations no self-respecting shepherd would use any crook other than those made in the forge at Pyecombe. Then the village craftsman died and left no apprentice capable of carrying on his work, though others tried to copy the style. The characteristic Pyecombe crook had a curve pulled almost into a semi-circle and then turned slightly back on itself. 'How difficult it is to describe so simple a matter as a shepherd's crook!' as Richard Jefferies so rightly observed. Inferior crooks might be too wide, so that a sheep could get its leg out; others were made of too soft an iron, and would bend; too tight a curve meant too small an opening, useful only for lambs. The craft must have been revived after Jefferies' day, for two skilled practitioners in one family are mentioned by Esther Meynell, writing in 1944. Today the forge still makes crooks – for bishops – but does a brisker trade in ornamental ironwork, gates, chess pieces and modern iron sculpture.

If Steyning is truly Chanctonbury's town, and Ditchling the deferential attendant to its Beacon, then Poynings and Fulking are surely inseparable from the Devil's Dyke. The Poynings family served the Crown with distinction from Norman times until the middle of the Tudor era. Michael Poynings was Guardian of the Sussex Coast in the mid-fourteenth century, fought at Crécy and returned safely to erect the church in which he is now buried. Edward Poynings was Henry VII's lord deputy in Ireland. When the family died out, Henry VIII presented the manor to his favoured Sir Anthony Browne; and, knowing what we do of the curse laid upon that family and its possessions, we are hardly surprised to learn that the house was later burnt down.

Fulking has a fountain drawn from a fine natural spring, dedicated to the memory of John Ruskin. It also has another source of refreshment. In a book such as this it would be impractical to attempt any assessment of eating and drinking establishments along our route, since changes of staff or ownership can alter such places out of all recognition within a matter of weeks. But I find it hard to believe that the *Shepherd and Dog* inn can ever go too seriously wrong.

Too many pleasant inns are, regrettably, in danger. As the major combines engulf yet another respected local brewery and replace characteristic local beers with that characterless fizz which a friend of mine aptly designates 'beer cordial', so they chivvy out the tenant landlords who have shaped the personality of their pubs and replace them with their own suitably trained, suitably impersonal managers. Where profits do not reach the level decreed by the monopoly's computer, every attempt is made to close the pub down and divert business to a chromium-plated neighbour; and if that nearest neighbour is seven or eight miles away, too bad for the loyal local. 'Change of use' is an innocuous little phrase used in applications to dispose of such premises – change of use meaning, usually, sale to some 'foreigner' wanting premises which can be tarted up into a week-end cottage.

The Devil's Dyke has the appearance of a vast slice of some inexplicable fortification. Any romantically concocted legend of a race of giants battling over its wall and the deep plunge of its vertiginous moat would be at least as plausible as the story which has clung to it for so long. It is said that the devil, worried that pagan Sussex should have been so swiftly transformed into 'Selig Sussex' – Holy Sussex and not, as some would have it, Silly Sussex – decided to take steps. He set to work one night to dig a channel through the Downs from the sea, so that the distasteful clusters of church towers and spires in the Weald might be drowned. He was an energetic devil, but not a very intelligent one. All it took to frighten him off was an old woman who, holding a candle up to her cottage window to see what all the activity was, set all the local cocks crowing in the conviction that dawn was breaking, a conviction shared by the fleeing devil.

In late Victorian times a light railway linked the dyke with Brighton. A hotel was built, with its own amusement park, and on one bank holiday the proprietor claimed that 30,000 people had passed through his grounds. There was also a funicular railway up the side of the ditch itself, traces of the engine house and double trackway being still identifiable; and a cable car made a dizzying trip right across the chasm between two steel towers.

After the Second World War there was an attempt to revive the entertainments business along the Devil's Dyke, with published plans for a full-scale windmill, a replica of an Egyptian temple set into the wall of the dyke, and other delights. Mercifully we have been spared this.

When we have crossed the Adur, our trackway takes us above Wiston Park to Chanctonbury Ring. The Shirley family built the Tudor manor house, went out on many incredible adventures from here, and are buried – such of them as returned safely – in the fourteenth-century church. The church also has a celebrated brass of Sir John de Braose, last of the family who had been lords of the Rape of Bramber. But it is a later owner of Wiston Park who is most fondly remembered here. If ever a man may be said to have set his seal on the landscape, it is Sir Charles Goring.

Goring was a fervent planter of trees. Much of the woodland between Steyning and Washington is his work. His pet project was that of crowning Chanctonbury with a ring of beeches. He planted them in 1760 when he was still at school and, living to be 85, lived to see them grow to maturity. If he had embarked on such a scheme today he might have been denounced as a vandal, perpetrating such an anachronism on this old Roman and Celtic site. But it is one of those personal whims which have succeeded. Chanctonbury without its Ring is now unthinkable: from far and near it is a landmark, a weather-vane, a consolation, a reference point for all that lies beside, beneath or beyond it.

The other great hump to the south is, in contrast, bare.
There is a good pathway from the South Downs Way towards
it, or it can be reached by a minor road out of Findon, sheltering – or cowering – in its little vale. Cissbury camp was
developed by successive tribes and cultures until it covered
60 acres, with an outer rampart forming an oval more than a
mile long. At one part the protecting wall crosses the group
of flint mines which belong to the earliest period of human
activity on the site. There is a wonderful confusion of races
here: Stone Age and Iron Age, Saxon upon Celt.

Findon contributes a Norman church with a flawless decorated arch, some well-worn wooden benches, and an aged
wooden screen. Its roof covers a double nave. Not far down
the road are Patching, whose church has some fine local ironwork, and Clapham, within whose church is one of the
country's finest brasses. It shows Sir John Shelley and his wife
Elizabeth, watched over by the Holy Trinity, and is accompanied by other brasses and memorials to the Shelley family,
forefathers of the poet.

Over the Downs again and down the northern scarp to
Storrington, or due west along the southern edges, we come
to the Arun; and, crossing it, find a marked change in the
character of the Downs themselves.

*   *   *

West of the Arun, the slopes and crests are more thickly
wooded, less uncompromising, one might almost say domesticated. In some ways these woodlands and gentle glades
seem to belong more to Hampshire and Surrey than to Sussex;
or is it that parts of Hampshire and Surrey belong in spirit
to Sussex?

From Houghton Forest over Bignor Hill and along the
northern slopes of Duncton, Woolavington, Graffham and
Heyshott Downs the trees cluster. Half-way up the steep
climb of the road out of Duncton towards Chichester is

a parking space generously donated and maintained for the benefit of those who wish to feast their eyes on the great goodness of the Weald and the forest ridge beyond. And in imagination perhaps we do hear Belloc as he wished we should hear him still – 'A boy that sings on Duncton Hill'.

On the farther side of the downland, too, there are riches, including the lovely parklands around Slindon. More than 3,000 acres of the Slindon estate, reaching right round to Bignor and Stane Street, are now administered by the National Trust. The park, with its famous beeches, is open daily, and elsewhere there are the most tempting footpaths. Part of the village comes under this administration.

Stephen Langton, the Archbishop of Canterbury who stood with the barons in their demand for the formulation of Magna Carta, died in the manor house here in 1228, and was taken to Canterbury for burial. In the church is a recumbent wooden effigy of a knight with his head resting on his helmet. He has lain here, his hands raised in prayer and his lips slightly parted in a wondering question, for some 400 years, and apart from a cleft in his brow shows little sign of deterioration.

In the villages below the Downs and on into the Weald there are many examples of the gable construction known as the 'Sussex hip'. Instead of allowing thatch or tile at the gable ends to descend as deeply as that along the main slopes of the roof, the builder 'hipped back' his roof to protect the apex of the gable and also allow space for an attic window in the end wall, simpler to insert than a dormer window.

Roads through the woods and dells sprout warning signs, indicate car parks, and threaten that horses are liable to cross. DANGER, RACE HORSES is an injunction which might well be borne in mind by those hurrying towards Goodwood enclosure anxious to lose money on those most treacherous of four-footed creatures.

The setting of the racecourse is incomparable. Like the

bridge of a ship, its grandstand rises clear of the great length of woodland behind it and looks straight out over the swoop and climb of rolling downland ahead. Racing was introduced here by the third Duke of Richmond in 1801 for the benefit of officers in the Sussex Militia, of which he was Colonel, and in the following year the public were admitted. A race called the Silver Cup was instituted, to be replaced by a Gold Cup event in 1812 and ultimately the Goodwood Cup, now one of the longest flat races in the season. Originally there was one meeting of three or four days each year, but now there are fixtures in May, July, August and September. Between 1948 and 1966 a motor racing track operated round the airfield perimeter, now used only for vehicle testing, driving instruction, and occasional veteran car rallies. The airfield itself is the home of a flying school and a flying club.

The first Duke of Richmond was the son of Charles II and one of his mistresses, the beautiful Louise de Queroualle. He bought a Jacobean house here in 1697, purely for use as a hunting lodge. It was the third of the line who, in the later part of the eighteenth century, really settled into Goodwood and engaged James Wyatt to design the present house, adding stables and kennels, planting acres of trees, and establishing the tradition of racing. He died in debt before the octagonal mansion could be completed as planned, but his successors have been thankful : the house is more manageable in its present form.

Through the death of a kinsman the dukedom became that of Richmond and Gordon, but all the Scottish possessions had to be sold off before the Second World War to meet estate duty and mortgage repayments. During the war the Goodwood buildings were used as a military hospital. Today the family live in one private wing, while offices for managing the estate's various business enterprises have been set up in the other wings. Restoration of the main rooms was carried out between 1968 and 1970, providing a worthy setting for the great collections of china, tapestries and paintings, including works by Canaletto, Lely, Reynolds and, inevitably here, Stubbs. Visitors are expected to savour the atmosphere to the full by including in their itinerary lunch, afternoon tea or supper, and on certain Saturdays there are formal dinner parties in the State apartments.

Close to the western corner of the racecourse is the Trundle – from the Old English *trendel*, a circle or hoop. In fact there is more than one circle. An aerial photograph taken in 1925 showed that within the massive outer wall of the known Iron Age fort was another, older formation. Investigation revealed that the site had been occupied far back in the Stone Age. A female skeleton from about 2000 B.C. was discovered where a Neolithic ditch and the Celtic rampart intersected. While digging was going on, remains of domestic animals, Celtic pottery and different kinds of timber were brought to light. It is clear that until its abandonment about 100 B.C. the camp must have been a populous centre, with substantial wooden fortifications and even houses within the walls. Later the great mound became known as St Roche's Hill, from a fifteenth-century chapel whose outline can also be identified. One of the convicted members of the Hawkhurst smuggling gang was hanged in chains from a gibbet on the hill in 1747.

A road along the little valley below the parks threads together a sequence of quiet villages whose inns, full during race meeting periods, are sleepy and cosy for most of the rest of the year, but never altogether neglected: footpaths and bridleways from the South Downs Way wander down towards their warmth and shelter. For generations their inhabitants have been in the employ of the dukes on the ridge above, and have had little to complain about in the situation. Cobbett, riding through and rightly supposing that every inch of land belonged either to the Duke of Richmond or to Lord Egremont of Petworth, was glad to note that the labourers got fair play : a turnip-hoer's snack consisted of 'a good lump

of household bread and not a very small piece of bacon', and
there was a pig at almost every labourer's house. The rural
rider thought their cottage gardens 'some of the very best
that I have seen in England'.

He would be able to say the same today. East Dean is still
a glow of colour behind its low flint walls, radiating from a
murky duckpond. It denies the claim of the other East Dean
or Eastdean, near Beachy Head, to be the one where Bishop
Asser met Alfred the Great, and has a King Alfred's Well in
the parish to back up its own claim.

A mile to the west, Charlton is more important than it
appears. It was the Charlton Hunt, one of the oldest established regular foxhunts in England, which lured the first Duke
of Richmond to the district and to the hunting lodge from
which so much else developed.

Another short stretch of road leads into Singleton, crammed up against the main Midhurst to Chichester road but
peaceable in itself, with diminutive bridge and village green,
more flint cottages mellowed by red-tiled or thatched roofs,
and yet more luxuriant gardens. Towards the end of the nineteenth-century its tranquillity was shattered for brief periods
each year, when racegoers swarming into the neighbourhood
behaved as rowdily as present-day football crowds, until
action was taken by the local rector, residents, and the police.
The Prince of Wales, later Edward VII, stabled his horses here
and added a loftier note, echoed by the railway company
when they equipped their near-by station with waiting-room
carpets and a stained-glass window. Station and track are both
just a memory now.

The foxhunting fraternity are more lastingly remembered
in Singleton church. In 1744 died Thomas Johnson, who 'from
his early inclination to fox hounds ... soon became an experienced huntsman' and won 'the approbation of several of the
nobility', one of whom installed a large plaque with an affectionate inscription :

Here JOHNSON lies What Hunter can deny
Old, honest TOM the Tribute of a Sigh.
Deaf is that Ear, which caught the opening Sound,
Dumb is that Tongue, which cheer'd the Hills around.
Unpleasing Truth Death hunts us from our Birth
In view; and Men, like Foxes, take to Earth.

Also buried here is Sir Francis D'Arcy Cooper, who at his death in 1941 left the Drovers estate of over 1,000 acres to the National Trust. The local *Drovers Inn* had a long connection not with the movement of sheep but with the movements of smugglers, until bought by a member of the Egremont family and converted into a private residence.

Just outside the village is a Weald and Downland Open Air Museum. It follows the Scandinavian practice of assembling in one place old buildings in danger of neglect or destruction, accompanied by examples of ancient crafts, vehicles, and conjectural reconstructions. Some 40 buildings are planned for the site. At present the main show pieces are a fourteenth-century Kentish house, an eighteenth-century granary from Littlehampton, a toll cottage from Beeding, and a Hampshire tread-wheel for winding up buckets from a deep well. A re-created charcoal burner's camp recalls the iron and gunpowder industries of the Weald.

In setting up one of the old houses as authentically as possible, the rebuilders found themselves in trouble with the consistency of the daub needed to bind the wattles together. It shrank or expanded according to the weather, and refused to hold. Some fragments of the original were analysed by a Ministry of Agriculture chemist, from which the correct mix was calculated. The key ingredient proved to be a large quantity of liquid cow dung. 'We cheated a bit, though', came the wry confession: 'instead of mixing it by hand in the old-fashioned way, we decided to use a cement mixer'.

From this spacious museum, with its nature trail and

woodland walks, there is a fine view of the great flint mansion of West Dean. It was here that Edward VII stayed when attending race meetings. Today it has been turned into a residential college for the teaching of old and new British crafts, open to students of varying skills, a most suitable neighbour for the open air collection on the green slopes.

West Dean village runs along a short street parallel with the main road. Its grey little church has Saxon remnants in its walls, including a Saxon arch on the north wall of the nave, but a lot was damaged during a fire in 1934. The arch itself was blistered by the heat, and one old occupant of the church had to be removed: the seventeenth-century alabaster monument to three Richard Lewknors – father, son and grandson – lost the recumbent senior, so that only son and grandson are still in place, heads reverently bowed.

There is another monument in a church across that main road. The Stoughton tomb in West Stoke, with a sprightly robin atop, is really too massive for its setting, and crowded with figures. Adrian Stoughton, M.A. (he is wearing his gown), kneels at a desk with his wife Mary. They 'lived together in holy wedlock 31 years, happy parents of 16 children', seven of whom are depicted kneeling, some holding skulls of the nine others who 'died young'.

Stoke Clump rises above the hollow like a miniature Chanctonbury. Close at hand is the nature reserve of Kingley Vale, some 350 acres containing a wide variety of chalk downland plants and animals. Over 70 species of bird have been recorded, and there are deer, foxes and badgers. Its yew forest is all of 500 years old, and legend tells of an earlier plantation being laid out to celebrate the defeat by Chichester men of the Vikings in A.D. 895. Up to the time of Elizabeth I the yew was a protected tree, much valued as the provider of the finest longbow staves; but the gnarled old trunks here would be unlikely to yield the straight, supple lengths required.

Paths through the vale lead up towards a great concentration of ancient mounds and diggings. On Bow Hill are Bronze Age bell and bowl barrows, dubbed locally the Devil's Humps. Looking down into the valley, it is not difficult to make out the patterns of Celtic lynchets, marked now by grassy banks. There are flint mines and, farther on towards Chilgrove, the double concentric ramparts of Goosehill camp. And yet farther, between Chilgrove and Elsted, there are five bell-shaped barrows on Treyford Hill which, in competition with those on Bow Hill, are known as the Devil's Jumps. The devil is obviously considered by Sussex folk to be a very active character.

Another figure of some local repute, the giant Bevis, has left his mark in the shape of Bevis's Thumb, a long barrow above the Mardens, a scattering of little hamlets close to the Hampshire border.

In contrast to these rough prehistoric relics are the landscaped grounds and house of Uppark, with its attendant folly, summerhouse, dairy and game larder. The house was built at the end of the seventeenth century and the beginning of the eighteenth, on foundations which date from the fifteenth century. There was certainly some kind of house on the site during the time of Charles I, when the owner of Uppark and of the manor of Harting was Sir Edward Ford, inventor of the first effective water pump. He was unable to hold Arundel for the king, but seems to have been well treated by Cromwell, who appointed him First Lord of the Works, a position he was allowed to retain when Charles II came to the throne. His grandson, Lord Grey of Werke, was an even more assiduous imitator of the Vicar of Bray than Sir Edward had been. Accused of high treason because of his intrigues with the Duke of Monmouth, he managed by a ruse to escape incarceration in the Tower of London, ran off with Lady Henrietta Berkeley to the Netherlands to join Monmouth, and came back to command the ill-fated duke's cavalry at Sedgemoor.

Yet when handed over to James II he was not sent off to the Tower, not tried by his peers, and certainly not thrown into the clutches of the appalling Judge Jeffreys. Having sought pardon and paid a large indemnity, he was granted the king's confidence; but made haste to associate himself with William III on that king's arrival in England, and duly became Lord Privy Seal.

He had been fickle in other matters, too. Shortly before the Monmouth rebellion he had seduced his wife's sister and, in spite of a lawsuit which went against him, refused to return her to her father. It was this sister, Lady Henrietta, whom he took with him when he went to join Monmouth on the Continent.

Respectable again and in royal favour, he set about building the new Uppark, using as architect William Talman, Comptroller of the King's Works. After his death the estate passed to his daughter, whose grandson sold it to Sir Matthew Fetherstonhaugh. The Fetherstonhaughs carried out major changes to the house and its outbuildings and introduced many of the finest pieces of furniture and works of art now on display in the dining-room, parlours and drawing-rooms, and in the beautiful saloon which was their creation.

Their son Harry brought something even more remarkable into Uppark. Enamoured of a beautiful 15-year-old dancer at the Temple of Aesculapius in London, he carried her off to his home, along with her illegitimate baby. She was his mistress for a year. There is a table in the house on which Sir Harry made her dance for him. She was expecting another child when he decided to dismiss her. With very little delay she was taken up by Charles Greville, who had met her while shooting at Uppark, painted many times by Romney, and in due course handed over to Sir William Hamilton, with whom she lived for five years before becoming Lady Hamilton. After another seven years or so she met Lord Nelson. When that historic love affair ended with the great admiral's death, she

Here Lyeth the Body
of FRANSES Wife of
THOMAS PORTER
Gent. and Daughter
of Sr WILLIAM
COLEPEPYR BARt
of Aylsford in
KENT
Who Died October
the 18 1717
Aged 79

And
MARY ALCRON
Her Daughter
by A Former
Husband

sank into destitution, but some spark of affection must have kindled again, for Sir Harry did get in touch after a long silence and several times paid off her debts.

Many of the Fetherstonhaughs are remembered in the church at South Harting, the village north of the park, where Anthony Trollope lived and worked for some years.

Another author who had connections with the district was H. G. Wells. For 13 years his mother was housekeeper at Uppark, and Wells spent most of his youth there.

Ownership of the property had by now undergone a remarkable change. The Sir Harry who had once been Emma Hart's lover and, after her departure, a great man-about-town and friend of the Prince Regent, decided at the age of 70 that it was time he got married. As bride he chose his head dairymaid, Mary Ann Bullock, and sent her off to Paris to be properly educated. Whatever crude jokes and insinuations may have been bandied about the village, Sir Harry discountenanced them all by living on contentedly with his wife for another 21 years. He also made her younger sister Frances welcome in his household, and paid for her to have a similar education. This proved a wise move, for after his death and his widow's eventual death it was Frances who inherited. She took the Fetherstonhaugh name and lived decorously on at Uppark with a lady companion who had once been her governess, both of them unvaryingly dressed in black. This was the background which Wells recalled in his autobiography, and which he fictionalised in his novel *Tono-Bungay*.

Having rounded Beacon Hill – though there is nothing to stop the more energetic from climbing right over it – the last section of the South Downs Way in this county crosses the Uppark estate by Tower Hill and on over the South Harting to Compton road. There we must let it go, on into Hampshire and the Queen Elizabeth Forest, while we turn back into Sussex.

24 *Wealden iron in Wadhurst Church*

CHAPTER FIVE

The Western Weald

Dividing the Downs from the Weald makes geological sense, even with so many villages, estates and lanes pulling the two together again and blurring the boundaries. It is more difficult to treat the northern Forest Ridge as a separate entity, and I do not propose to try. Villages, crafts and farms are shared out between hills and Weald, overlapping and intermingling, and a route from one end of the county to the other will naturally wander in and out of both.

In the wooded north-west corner, with one foot trailing into Surrey, is a summit which lords it over any South Downs upstart. Black Down is, at 918 feet, the highest point in Sussex. Aldworth House, built on its slopes in 1868 by the poet who is remembered in Tennyson's Lane, faces towards Surrey, but in the quarter of a century he spent here until his death Tennyson must often have climbed Black Down to contemplate that other vista of

> *Green Sussex fading into blue*
> *With one grey glimpse of sea.*

Despite its nearness to Haslemere and the main London to Chichester road, and its popularity with walkers and riders, the region remains strangely private. The cottages of Fernhurst, Lurgashall and Lodsworth cluster around their village greens; churches are discreetly veiled by trees; the mill pond has forgotten what it is like to have to work for a living.

Yet we are looking out over what was once the busiest concentration of industry in Britain.

With the introduction of new glass-making techniques by Dutch and French settlers, Chiddingfold in Surrey became, in the thirteenth century, a prosperous centre of the craft, and these lessons were soon learnt in neighbouring Sussex. Furnaces were established near Kirdford, Petworth and Loxwood, and expanded with the arrival of Huguenot refugees in the sixteenth century. At one time there were so many of these in the district that services in Wisborough Green church were frequently conducted in French. Local sands proved ideal for glass manufacture, and the Wealden forests supplied ample fuel.

At least, for a while the supply was ample. Then the great Andredsweald forest shrank, denuded by shipbuilders, iron-founders and the glass-makers. The glass and iron trades found themselves at odds with each other, competing for dwindling supplies of charcoal. In 1616 the iron-masters won: an Act was passed forbidding the use of wood fuel in glass manufacture, thereby virtually abolishing the industry in this region.

The iron-masters were in every sense, over many centuries, masters of the Weald.

After the Romans had abandoned Britain, their scattered iron workings suffered the fate of so many of the legacies they had bequeathed to the colony: nobody had the will or energy to continue production. As for the incoming Saxon conquerors, they appear to have made no attempt whatsoever to make use of the natural resources or remaining equipment. In Domesday Book the Normans have only one reference to the subject, recording the existence of an iron mine near East Grinstead.

Extraction and production did not recommence until the middle of the thirteenth century, and received a terrific impetus in the fifteenth and sixteenth centuries, until Camden could declare Sussex

full of iron mines, all over it; for the
casting of which there are furnaces up and
down the country, and abundance of wood is

yearly spent; many streams are drawn into
one channel and a great deal of meadow
ground is turned into ponds and mills for
the driving of mills by the flashes, which,
beating with hammers upon the iron, fill
the neighbourhood about it, night and day
with continual noise.

The picture of central Sussex as a fiery, clanging Black
Country is hard to conjure up today. But the evidence is there,
in scores of local names : Hammer Pond House, Furnace Lane,
Iron House Cottage, Old Forge Lane, Cinder Hill.

Early furnaces were simple and wasteful. Known as bloo-
meries, from the blooms or crude ingots which came out at
the end of the process, they employed alternating layers of
charcoal and iron ore built up into a beehive mound. Encased
in clay, this was fired, and kept going by a bellows at the base.
Little progress had been made with the bellows since Roman
times : it was operated by foot, and produced insufficient
draught to maintain a consistently fierce blaze, so that the
soft 'plastic iron' collecting at the foot of the furnace was full
of impurities, and much that was worth extracting remained
in the cinders. Output was slow and small, and a family or
two could, without too much ambition, operate the whole
process much as they would work a smallholding.

In the fifteenth century new smelting techniques were introduced from France. They initiated an early Industrial
Revolution. Instead of small, individually assembled furnaces
which were broken up after each firing there had to be a permanent blast furnace, its powerful bellows operated by a
wheel, the wheel in its turn being driven by horse or oxen
power, or by water. The charcoal burned the iron ore at a
higher temperature, cleansing it more effectively of impurities
and producing increased quantities of metal. The improved

liquefaction made the iron easier to run off into moulds and to be fashioned as required.

To provide water power for these blast furnaces, ponds were dug and streams were dammed. They served a threefold purpose: water released from them worked the bellows, worked the hammers in the forges, and could be used to cool the iron and the workers' implements.

The useful life of these furnaces and forges was conditioned by fuel supplies in the vicinity. Once the surrounding region had been stripped bare, the iron-master and his men had to move on and start up a new factory elsewhere, for transport was poor and the expense of bringing wood or charcoal from any appreciable distance was prohibitive. As the years went on, it grew more and more difficult to find any unexploited patch of woodland.

The navy wanted Wealden oak for its ships. It also wanted guns for those ships. The two demands were counter-productive. Timber used in shipbuilding could not be used to fire the furnaces making the weapons; and vice versa.

Improvements in the manufacture of cannon contributed to the dilemma. Earlier types had been made of iron bars welded together and strengthened by iron hoops, offering as serious a peril to their own gunners as to the enemy. But in 1543, according to Holinshed,

> *Master Huggett and his man John*
> *They did make the first cannon.*

Some records give the name as Ralph Hogg, and the inventor's home, still there in Buxted, is called Hogge House. As for his man John, he must be there purely for the sake of the rhyme: Huggett's or Hogg's associate was actually Peter Baude, a French expert. Whatever minor discrepancies there may have been in the matter of names, however, there seems little doubt that these two men were responsible for the first iron cannon to be cast in one piece. Such guns were soon in demand not merely for our own naval forces but for those of potential enemies. When restrictions were imposed on exports which might be turned against the country in time of war, the time-honoured Sussex trade of smuggling came to the rescue of the arms profiteers.

Peter Baude also evolved a forerunner of the modern grenade. In collaboration with an inventive Dutchman, he

did cause to be made certain hollow shot
of cast iron to be stuffed with firework
or wild fire, where of the bigger sort
had screws or iron to receive a match to
carry the fire kindled, that the firework
might be set on fire for to break into
pieces the same hollow shot where of the
smallest piece hitting any man would
kill or spoil him.

When there was no patriotic obligation to kill or spoil men, the foundries forged iron for more peaceful purposes: ornamental gates and railings, firebacks, and gravestones.

And still the forests receded. The Privy Council was so alarmed by the 'great spoil and consumption of oaks and other woods in the counties of Sussex, Surrey and Kent' that it empowered an inspector to visit all the known ironworks and report on the rate of destruction. An Act was passed to control the felling of timber within 12 miles of the coast and so protect the needs of the Cinque Ports shipbuilders. Little attention seems to have been paid to this or any other edict. Then as now, immediate greed overruled long-term planning. There was unrelenting consumption; and almost no reafforestation. 'Abundance of wood', Camden had said. Not any longer.

Final collapse came with the exploitation of rich veins of

ore close to coal mines and their superior fuel in the north, Wales, and the Midlands. The Sussex furnaces ceased to blow. The banks of the hammer ponds ceased to reverberate. Small-scale production struggled on, but without hope of recapturing the once prosperous market. The last fire died at Ashburnham, in East Sussex, early in the nineteenth century.

Quite some time after this, an unemployed man named John Every led his wife and family out of the Weald to seek a new home and work in Lewes. In spite of the sad history of the industry's declining years he set up his own rudimentary iron foundry, and by dint of hard work and good management made a success of it. The firm was fond of boasting that it was responsible for Brighton being what it was, and the assertion was not far wrong : the piers and railings, the much-admired and nowadays much-photographed balconies adorning so many squares and terraces, all came from this Lewes foundry.

At the height of his success Every lost the entire place in a fire. By this time he must have established himself in the hearts of his fellow citizens, since they readily lent him money to start again. Rising from the ashes, his new venture was appropriately named The Phoenix Iron Works.

Less fortunate buildings had decayed long before, yet have left certain imprints on the landscape, more attractive than most industrial residue. The loveliest relics are the tranquil hammer ponds, reflecting the trees which have been allowed to cluster round them again, often approached by narrow lanes gouged deeply out of the earth by the iron dragged through them when the Weald was still very much the Wild; lanes so deep and shadowy that even on a windy day the lower leaves of the hedges do not so much as whisper. There are ponds in St. Leonard's Forest, around Slaugham, and by the lovely spring gardens of Leonardslee, near Lower Beeding. Veins of iron emerge on the surface of many an ancient path, beside old watermill buildings near Mayfield, and on the heathland of Ashdown Forest. Deposits of cinders are revealed when a neglected ditch dries up. The Sussex Naturalists' Trust have a nature trail through Nap Wood, a few miles from Rotherfield, which incorporates an Iron Age trackway prob-ably connected with the earliest period of iron working in the county.

And always, of course, there are the resonant names: Cinderfield, Beckley Furnace, Chimneys. We can trace how the glass-making communities, deprived of fuel for the benefit of the iron workers, made the best of a bad job by taking up that trade themselves. Around Fernhurst, Kirdford and their old associates there appear Hammer Patches, Minepit Close and Furnace Wood.

That particular little cluster of villages which once readily accepted instruction from foreign craftsmen came under the influence of a different kind of teacher in the middle of the last century.

In a presumably unconscious emulation of St Cuthman, who conveyed his mother to Steyning by cart, a 30-year-old evangelist named John Sirgood arrived in Sussex from London in 1850, pushing a handcart which contained his possessions and, whenever she grew footsore, his wife. Sirgood had been a follower of the faith-healing, puritanical doctrines of the Plumstead Peculiars, and, having himself taken up preaching, decided to strike out into the countryside. At Loxwood he must have received some sign as significant as that which had brought St Cuthman to a halt, for here he decided to stay.

To the local inhabitants he preached the necessity of plain living and renunciation. All must be dependent on Christ; and when he had gathered a large enough body of supporters, he named his sect the Society of Dependants. They must read no books but the Bible, allow no frivolous decorations in their homes – not even flowers – and indulge themselves in no sport or entertainment. A meeting-house and graveyard were established at Loxwood, and Sirgood acquired disciples as far away as Chichester.

At some stage the members of the society became known as Cokelers, perhaps because cocoa was their permitted beverage, or perhaps from the corruption of some local place name now lost to us.

The group acquired considerable power in its family of villages. Local stores were run by the Cokelers on co-operative principles; at Loxwood there was a bakery; and they operated a pioneer taxi in the neighbourhood. Dressed soberly in black, they prayed mightily, and at their meetings testified somewhat in the Quaker manner. Their descendants still own the shops and garages, and some still try to maintain their austere way of life in a world which offers their children too many temptations. They are no longer quite so self-contained, quite so obviously set apart; and it seems unlikely that their ascetic practices will survive another generation.

For such calculatedly withdrawn people the outside world must have been bounded by Midhurst and Petworth. And when Sirgood founded his society, those two little townships were themselves quiet places, and remained so until well into this century. E. V. Lucas could write of Midhurst that, being on no great highway, it was nearly always quiet. 'Nothing ever hurries there. The people live their own lives, passing along their few narrow streets and the one broad one, under the projecting eaves of timber houses, unreacking of London and the world'. Busy highways now converge on it, and in the narrow streets the pedestrian has to stand well back as traffic manoeuvres, jolts, and comes to a seething halt.

Midhurst remains, nevertheless, an inviting town, set trimly above the western Rother on its way to join the Arun. There are leisurely walks along the river and in the parklands and woods to the north. Cowdray Park, with the gutted ruins of Sir Anthony Browne's old house and with its growing contemporary fame as a setting for polo tournaments, opens out spaciously from the end of that one broad street Lucas mentioned. For the weary, there is the hospitality of the fine old *Spread Eagle* hotel. Parts of this, like the church across the road, are of fifteenth-century vintage. The church still rings curfew at eight o'clock every evening. This is said to be the sequel to the events of one dark night when a lonely rider, hopelessly lost, was able to get his bearings again by the sound of Midhurst's church bell. He thereupon bought a patch of land in the town and presented it to the community in return for a guarantee that the curfew bell would be rung every night thenceforth. The gift is now known as Curfew Garden. The bell is also traditionally sounded at noon every Shrove Tuesday.

Richard Cobden, the fourth of eleven children, was born near by in 1804, attended the grammar school in Midhurst, and returned to the district to settle at the end of his distinguished public career. His birthplace was a farmhouse between Heyshott and Cocking Causeway, from which he was sent in due course to be brought up by relations in Yorkshire. He became one of the leading spirits of the Anti-Corn Law League and an untiring advocate of free trade. In 1841 he entered Parliament and in the company of John Bright, a Quaker cotton manufacturer from Rochdale who sat as M.P. for Durham, spoke fluently against all protectionist restrictions. The Corn Laws were repealed in 1846. In 1860 Cobden negotiated a treaty with France which effected a mutually advantageous reduction in many tariffs. By now he was feeling the strain, physically and financially. In the pursuit of his ideals he had neglected his own business and was in danger of bankruptcy. A grateful nation subscribed to a fund with which he retired to build Dunford House on the land where his old home had once stood. Some of his school books and other mementoes are kept in the house. He is buried near by at West Lavington, and there is an obelisk in his memory by Cocking Causeway. There is also a pub called the *Richard*

Cobden Arms at Cocking, which changed hands in 1972 and gave rise to some alarm when there were rumours of 'change of use'. Happily it was still functioning normally when I last passed that way.

The truly appreciative traveller really ought to cut down to a saunter here. It is impossible to recommend any specific route; and equally impossible to advise against any particular turning. Selham and Graffham have attractive churches in attractive settings, but not of such importance as to warrant an earnest pilgrimage. The thing to do is to wander, weaving towards the river and away from it. There are spacious commons, unexpected tracts of heather beyond the clusters of woodland, and that perfect backdrop of the Downs towards Duncton. No hurry: essential that there should be no hurry.

Wild flowers seem to be coming back along the verges of these amiable little roads, as though to deny a recent indignant accusation by the Sussex Rights of Way Group that 'every last weed and flower was being sprayed out of existence . . . time an effort was made to add some colour and variety to the dreary verges on both major and lesser roads'.

Across this unflurried river valley we can, on foot, come upon Petworth almost unawares. By car it will have to be by rejoining one of the main roads. The one from Midhurst and Easebourne does at least offer the pleasures of Cowdray Park on either side.

Petworth has cobbled streets which ought surely to be made pedestrian precincts rather than, as one was on my last visit, an impromptu car park; which is not to say that I advocate spoiling the architectural colour schemes of the town by introducing a rash of double yellow lines. Like Arundel, this humped, hilly little town is worth more than just a ten-minute stroll as an adjunct to the ritual tour of Petworth House. One imagines it at its best on a sunny midsummer day when by some miracle all the approach roads have been sealed off and the place left to its own devices – always provided that the local shops have been well stocked in anticipation.

The parish church of Our Lady of Pity was restored in haphazard fashion by Sir Charles Barry in the nineteenth century and a brick spire added, arousing a lot of criticism until replaced in 1953 by a type of Sussex cap. Some of the other damage was readjusted by a more circumspect restorer in 1902. There is modern painted glass by Ninian Comper; and, ancient and modern, inscriptions to the families who have in turn owned Petworth House, starting with the Percys.

William de Percy came from France with the Conqueror in 1066 and was well rewarded. Among Saxon lands presented to him were those of the Earl of Northumbria, whose daughter Percy married. Direct succession to these estates was broken by the death of the third male in the original line at Jerusalem during the First Crusade, leaving only two daughters. The younger of these married the brother of Henry I's widow. The king had left Queen Adeliza the manor of Petworth, which she now presented to her brother, who took the Percy name and became Lord of Petworth and Castellan of Arundel. Later the earldom of all Northumberland was conferred upon the family. Petworth was more than once to provide a welcome retreat for the earls from the consequences of dangerous Court intrigue and perpetual skirmishes along the Border.

The earliest house would have been of no great size. No records survive giving comprehensive details of it, but it is known that in 1309 permission was sought to crenellate it. Later owners included Harry Hotspur, whose sword, taken from his dead hand at Shrewsbury, is kept in the present house. His widow is glowingly preserved in brass beside her second husband, Lord Camoys, in Trotten church, the other side of Midhurst. (They are in the company of Margaret Camoys, represented in the first brass known to have pictured a woman). They were violent times: of eleven successive earls, seven died violent deaths or went to prison, and few attempted any ambitious changes to their Sussex property.

The sixth earl, a well-educated young man of generously romantic tastes, though poor in health, might have done more if his life had not been embittered by a hopeless love affair and near-disgrace. At the age of 20 he fell in love with the daughter of Henry viii's Treasurer of the Household, and she reciprocated his feelings for long enough to get them both into trouble.

She was Anne Boleyn, who by then had probably come to the king's notice. As for young Henry Percy, he knew that his father had as good as settled a dynastic marriage for him with the Earl of Shrewsbury's daughter, and that the king tacitly approved of this. Nevertheless he and Anne made no secret of their mutual infatuation, until the king instructed Cardinal Wolsey to discipline Percy, at that time completing his education in the cardinal's household. There was a violent clash between prelate and protégé, resulting in the young man's father being summoned to London to take him away. The marriage of convenience took place but soon broke up, in a torrent of mutual recrimination. One wonders what Henry Percy's emotions were eight years later when, now himself Earl of Northumberland, he was the one commanded to arrest Wolsey on a charge of high treason; and whether Wolsey thought how much better off he would have been if he had encouraged rather than blocked a marriage between Percy and Anne Boleyn. When the time for Anne's own arrest and trial came, Northumberland sat as one of her judges and, after the verdict had been announced, collapsed. He died the following year – of a broken heart, it has been said.

At some time the original house was abandoned and another one built, to be enlarged by the eighth earl. It was the ninth earl who had the most ambitious plans for it, but he was unable to carry them out because of lack of funds:

having spent 16 years in the Tower suspected of complicity in the Gunpowder Plot, he had to pay a huge fine in order to win his release and pardon. He devoted the remaining 11 years of his life, shut away at Petworth, to experiments in alchemy and other pseudo-sciences, which led to his becoming known as the Wizard Earl. Perhaps he hoped to create his own supply of gold to further his architectural dreams.

His son drew up further plans, but he too was unable to develop them. Between them, however, they managed to collect many of the pictures which now enrich every room in the present building. Van Dyck painted the son Algernon in a family group with his wife and daughters, and did a fine posthumous study of the Wizard Earl. Both of these hang in the square dining-room with several other Van Dycks and some by Lely.

The second Percy line came to an end in 1670, leaving one girl, Elizabeth, who became the pawn in a game of arranged marriages. She was wed three times before she was 16. The first two marriages were unhappy and she tried to run away, but in each case had her sorrows more effectively eased by widowhood. Her third husband was the sixth Duke of Somerset, regarded by most of his own circle as insufferably arrogant. He was certainly accustomed to getting his own way, and imposed his own ideas on the house and town. As soon as his wife came of age he commandeered her fortune to rebuild Petworth on a lavish scale.

With the aid of an architect whose identity has never been satisfactorily confirmed, though he is thought to have been French, Somerset demolished most of the old house, retaining only the thirteenth-century Percy chapel. The new frontage was more than 300 feet long, and although it was remodelled in the last century it remains true to its original concept. Its uncompromising four-square regularity – rectangularity, perhaps – was at first offset by a central dome, but this was removed by the third Lord Egremont.

Inside, each room is a treasure chest. The 'Proud Duke' ensured that his personal splendour should not be forgotten – there is an allegorical mural showing his wife in triumph with their children, the duke's heraldic supporters of bull and unicorn in marble appear over the chimney-pieces in the Marble Hall, and the Beauty Room has an assembly of titled ladies who were his wife's friends at Court– but at the same time he ensured that the settings should be worthy of the paintings and furniture he inherited or collected. Nowhere is this more evident than in the Grinling Gibbons room.

Given his head, the great wood-carver created a lime-wood cornucopia of fruit and flowers, an exuberance of birds and beasts, leaping, twining and singing to the accompaniment of exquisitely wrought musical instruments. With its view out over park and lake, this is surely the richest room in the great, long house. Among the florid carvings which frame the portraits, including several by Lely and Reynolds, the great craftsman reserved his most sumptuous efforts for the duke himself, surrounding him with coronets, victor's spoils and every possible grandiose embellishment.

In the town the family name is associated with Somerset Lodge, a perfect little stone house, and the almshouses of Somerset Hospital. Gibbons stayed at New Grove Lodge while working on his unforgettable Carved Room.

Proud the sixth Duke of Somerset may have been of his noble line, but it fared no better than that of the Percys. The seventh left only one daughter, who married a London physician. It was agreed that the estates should not be left exclusively to her but divided with a nephew. The physician followed the now familiar practice of changing his name to Percy, and was given the earldom and certain Northumbrian estates, while others including Petworth and the earldom of Egremont went to the nephew, Charles Wyndham.

It is the third Lord Egremont we remember with most gratitude. He assembled the collection of works by Romney,

Gainsborough, Holbein and Rembrandt. He was a generous host and a discerning patron of writers and painters. Admiring Turner especially, he provided the artist with a studio here. One whole room of the house is now devoted to Turner's work. Among the paintings on show are two scenes in the adjoining park, and a haunting, hazy, golden picture of the old Chichester Canal. This recalls Egremont's enthusiasm for canals, his work on behalf of the Rother Navigation and of the Wey and Arun project, and his tireless concern with the prosperity of his tenants and employees as much as with his own.

Yet again we find a line facing extinction. The third Lord Egremont was not merely enlightened but what we might call permissive. He lived happily enough for some years with a mistress who was accorded by everyone the courtesy of Mrs Wyndham. She bore him six children, after which he belatedly decided to marry her. They then produced no legitimate offspring, so the title passed to a nephew and died out. The oldest son, who inherited the actual estates, was created Lord Leconfield. It was the third of this name who gave Petworth House to the National Trust, and again a nephew appears on the scene – John Wyndham, who in 1963 became Lord Egremont in a new creation.

The river below Petworth leads on between a diversity of little streams and runnels to Fittleworth, with its long street of snug, pretty houses and an old inn which could well have done without its modernisation but is still none too disquieting. Its attractive double bridge cannot, however, compare with that of Stopham, a short distance downstream.

Stopham church stands on a windy knoll, trees rustling unceasingly about it, with a neighbouring mansion and a cluster of stone cottages, warmed by an iridescence of hydrangeas. A riot of marble, stone and brass plaques within the church commemorate the military, legal, spiritual and temporal prowess of innumerable members of the local

25 *Bodiam Castle*

26   *The Preacher's House, Ewhurst*
27   *The Yeoman's House, Bignor*

Barttelot family. The walls are weighted with them, but the floors provide the more remarkable exhibition: below protective carpets, along nave and chancel, is a fantastic clutter of memorial brasses, large and small, to this prolific Norman family.

The Barttelots were united by marriage with the Stophams, of Saxon origin. The Stophams had long had the monopoly of dues on the ford over the river, but early in the fourteenth century the Barttelots built a bridge. It is a beauty. The central of its seven arches was raised in 1822 to allow barge traffic through, but this has not spoilt the lovely proportions of the bridge. Only the traffic of our time might conceivably do that. It would be enjoyable to stand meditatively in one of the embrasures above the water: enjoyable, were it not for single-file progress over the hump by cars and lorries with only inches to spare, controlled at each end by traffic lights. In 1968 flood waters rose high above the banks and the parapets, almost submerging the traffic lights and climbing far up the inn sign by the road. The inn has some alarming photographs of this. But even more alarming is its photograph of a 100-ton load being carried across the medieval span by transporter – surely too monstrous a burden to impose on such a venerable old charmer.

Crossing the bridge, we have once again crossed the Arun.

* * *

By Pulborough the Arun describes that wavering loop which the canal and Hardham tunnel were designed to by-pass. I stayed briefly in Pulborough during the war, and if asked for my recollections would have been able to say little more than that it was pleasant enough, but nothing special. I have found no later reason to change this opinion. Its best features are its landmark of a church, with an attractive old lych-gate, and its water meadows, with little channels from the river winding close up to the inns on the main road. There was once a Roman station on Stane Street, and relics of their occupation dug up at various times are kept in the church tower.

The church at West Chiltington is rich with wall paintings from the twelfth and thirteenth centuries. The village itself has opted for the twentieth, expanding into a sprawl of expensive modern houses and bungalows, and renovating older properties into what look like any other commuters' conversions – none the less bright, and neatly landscaped.

Thakenham has a church in which St Wilfrid, who taught Selsey men to fish, shares a window with St Francis and his birds.

If we turn back towards Stane Street we are carried straight, very straight indeed, into Billingshurst. It has been suggested that it owes its name to Belinus, the Roman engineer responsible for the highway, but there are also thought to have been Billingas in the region in Saxon times, and the Saxons were not in the habit of adopting anything left over by the Romans. But then, what are we to make of the fact that Stane Street's termination in London was close to what we call Billingsgate?

The River Adur, still a stripling, broadens a bit by Coolham, a clutch of houses about a crossroads. William Penn used to speak at Quaker meetings in the house called the Blue Idol, striding across the fields from Warminghurst and often devising a sermon on his way. The house was later enlarged and is still used for meetings of the Society of Friends, with an accompanying guest-house. Its strange name may have resulted from the incorporation of a ship's figurehead in its original timbers, or from the fact that parts of it were painted blue and that it was 'idle' through many years of disuse.

Four or five miles on along the main road, Cowfold church has a large brass to a prior of St Pancras at Southover, and a modest little one to a churchwarden.

It is a region of conflicting sects and doctrines: Roman, Reformation, Dissenting. Some of the more interesting facets are to be found well away from that main road, tucked away in a twisted little nest of lanes. At Shipley is a church founded by the Knights Templar, handed over to the Knights of St John after the Templars' downfall, and cared for by them until the Reformation. Among its post-Reformation tombs are those of the most influential Catholic family in the district, the Carylls. There are also windows in memory of the Burrells, whose prosperity rested on the profits of the iron industry. And there is a modern window whose design incorporates the celebrated windmill.

Church and windmill dominate Shipley; yet 'dominate' is too harsh a word. Say, rather, that they have established and now maintain its proportions. Hilaire Belloc came to the village, fell in love with it, bought the mill and settled in the house next door. From one viewpoint the cap and sails of the mill, now preserved as a monument to Belloc's memory, seem barely able to lift themselves above a windbreak of trees leading on down a shady, roughly flagged lane. But the face it turns towards the Downs is clear and proud.

It was this sweep of the Downs which captivated another newcomer, the composer John Ireland. Cheshire by birth, in 1920 he took a cottage in Ashington from which he could be sure of seeing Chanctonbury Ring, and came from London to stay in it as often and for as long as he could. Sussex was the source of many of his compositions, including *Amberley Wild Brooks*. In 1953 he settled in a converted windmill, still within sight of Chanctonbury. When he died in 1962 he was buried in Shipley churchyard in a grave marked by sarsen stones, 'to symbolise that antiquity the love of which inspired much of his music'. And from here, too, there is still that cherished view of the beech ring.

Wilfred Scawen Blunt, the poet who managed in his lifetime to embrace both the Mohammedan and Roman Catholic faiths, lived for some time near by at Newbuildings.

In St Mary's church there is also a memorial tablet to Annie

Ahlers, the actress who was killed in an accident in London, with an inscription written by Hilaire Belloc.

In the parkland below the church are Knepp castles old and new. The first is as toothy and forlorn as that other stronghold erected by the de Braose lords of Bramber : it was partially demolished by King John during his conflict with rebellious barons, and further reduced by Cromwell. Stones and rubble were later carted off for use in local road-building. A second castle arose in the early years of this century as home for the Burrells, still faithful to the neighbourhood. Knepp Pond is a wide, splendid lake : if it ever really was a hammer pond, as tradition has it, then it must have been the largest ever made.

Some miles away to the south-east the Adur swells in importance, and outside Henfield one of its meandering tributaries once drove a watermill. Woods Mill now houses an educational display of natural history material, related to the self-guiding trail through the adjacent 15-acre nature reserve.

Continuing south, we are confronted by the Downs. Northwards lies Horsham, one of the most substantial market towns in the county, and once an administrative centre almost equal in importance to Chichester or Lewes.

One road into the town takes us past Christ's Hospital. Famous as the Bluecoat School because of the blue gown worn by boy pupils, it was founded by Edward VI in about 1560. The original buildings in Newgate, London, were gutted in the Great Fire and rebuilt by Sir Christopher Wren. In 1672 the Mathematical School was established by Charles II, largely on the prompting of Samuel Pepys, with a view to providing boys with fundamental training which would enable them to qualify as naval officers. A commemorative painting by Verrio of the foundation ceremony hangs in the present dining hall.

Towards the end of the nineteenth century it grew increasingly evident that the premises were inadequate, and various sites outside central London were considered. In 1902, after some controversy, the school transferred to grounds outside Horsham. The buildings designed by Sir Aston Webb and Ingress Bell incorporated many Wren features, including the original gateway, which was dismantled and reassembled as part of the wall of Big School.

'This house is happy in its race of men', declares the motto; and among distinguished old boys depicted in the chapel are Lamb, Coleridge, and Leigh Hunt. In the quadrangle is a lead statue of the founder, Edward VI.

In any village along any route into Horsham are to be found roofs, such as that on the Blue Idol at Coolham, which at first glance appear alien to Sussex. Thatch and red tile give way unexpectedly to heavy grey stone, known as Horsham slabs. A large part of the town itself looks as if it could have been hewn from that same quarry.

Horsham's importance owed a lot to what some might consider the dubious advantage of being chosen to house the County Assizes in 1307. The courts functioned here until 1830, and in consequence there was also a succession of county gaols and 'houses of correction' over the centuries. Good money was to be made from the provision of food and accommodation when the judges were in session; money to be made from the prisons and prisoners, administered as they were by gaolers open to bribes from within and without; and even better pickings when there were executions, as there so frequently were. Horsham Hang Fairs were popular occasions, always held on a Saturday, when huge crowds would flock in to celebrate, and local tradesmen did roaring business with refreshments and souvenirs. The last public execution here was that of the murderer of a Brighton police superintendent in 1844. The Assize was now held at Lewes, but the county gaol had not yet been shifted, and it was in its condemned cell that the killer was lodged to await his last hour. Coster-mongers and cheapjacks from far afield made the most of this last event of its kind, ballad sellers hawked their wares through the crowd, pickpockets and tricksters of every persuasion sought their victims, and 'old Whiting at his beer shop nearly opposite the gaol was doing a roaring trade and expressing a wish that a man might be hanged every day'.

The various prisons were all set fairly close to the centre of the town, so that the area became known as Gaol Green, now amalgamated with the Carfax.

This name, which has appeared in some fascinating variations such as Scarfolks, Scarefolkes and Scar-fox, each open to interesting interpretation or misinterpretation, derives from the Latin *quadrifurcus* – four-forked, and thus a crossroads. The Horsham version may have come into use via a Norman corruption of *carrefour*, with the same meaning.

The Carfax has always been the hub of the town. Once it had a bull ring, stocks and a pillory. In 1891 a bandstand was constructed to provide worthier entertainment. It looks as though it might have strayed here from some faded inland spa, redolent with Strauss waltzes; and present conditions would defy all but the most brazen-lunged brass instrumentalist to make himself heard.

Beyond the Town Hall, the Causeway culminates in the soaring shingled spire and Horsham slab roof of the parish church. This wide street with its massive stone flags remains somehow detached from the rest of the town, shielded from it by the wedge of buildings blotting out Carfax, so that in spite of architectural changes one can still visualise those eighteenth-century afternoons when it was a fashionable promenade for leisured ladies and gentlemen.

Causeway House is now a museum, with one room devoted to Sussex iron, and displays relating to horse transport (with a collection of more horse bits than the trendiest green-belt pub could ever hope to amass), old bicycles and tricycles, and ship models.

The Normans built a church by the river, but it lasted only about a hundred years. A few traces of it can be found in the west and north-west of the present building, finished about 1247 and dedicated to St Mary the Virgin. Then a clerestory was added, brightening the painted beams and bosses of the wagon roof. The breadth and airiness of the whole interior are emphasised by the lack of a chancel arch.

In one of the chapels there is a Shelley vault, and a plaque to Percy Bysshe Shelley in the tower; though nothing in his life or expressed opinions would indicate that he wished any memento of himself to be preserved in this or any other place of Christian worship.

Shelley was born in 1792 at Field Place in the parish of Warnham, just outside Broadbridge Heath, now an undistinguished suburb of Horsham. After early tuition by the vicar of Warnham he was sent away to school, including an unhappy spell at Eton, and thereafter returned to Field Place only for solitary, introspective holidays. Sir Timothy Shelley had no sympathy for any of his son's ideas; and it is clear that the boy had none for his father's. When he was sent down from Oxford after publication of *The Necessity of Atheism*, Sir Timothy forbade him to come home, and they were not reconciled until after the poet's second marriage, when Sir Timothy settled a small income on him.

His cremation on an Italian shore was perhaps more fitting than interment in Horsham or Warnham would have been. But there are many other Shelleys at Warnham, including his own son.

Also at Warnham are more of the Jacobite Caryll family whose relations lie at Shipley. Sir John Caryll here was another of the mighty iron-masters, and in the family chapel is a window featuring Tubal-cain, the Biblical blacksmith and 'instructor of every artificer in brass and iron'.

Historic figures and events most vividly recorded and remembered tend to be those with a strong element of tragedy, murder or horror of one kind and another. Happy families, as Tolstoy pointed out, do not supply the most dramatic stories. But it is a pleasure to find in Warnham the tribute to one happy man with the gift for sharing that happiness with his fellows. He was Michael Turner, a contemporary of Shelley, who came from far humbler origins than the poet, did not ever venture so far afield, and seems to have been all the better for it. For 50 years he served as parish clerk and sexton, and led the choir. At every local festivity he was summoned to play the violin. He was also the local cobbler. When too old to sustain all these activities any longer, he was presented with a cottage by his fellow villagers, and they made sure that he lacked nothing for the rest of his life. He died clutching the violin from which he had drawn so much melody. It was lodged in the church, and the lord of the manor wrote his epitaph :

> *His duty done, beneath this stone*
> *Old Michael lies at rest;*
> *His rustic rig, his song, his jig*
> *Were ever of the best.*
>
> *With nodding head the choir he led*
> *That none should start too soon;*
> *The second, too, he sang full true,*
> *His viol played the tune.*
>
> *And when at last his age had passed*
> *One hundred less eleven,*
> *With faithful cling to fiddle string*
> *He sang himself to heaven.*

Between Horsham and Crawley is St Leonard's Forest, reaching out to join Tilgate Forest, on into East Sussex.

There were once two chapels of St Leonard in the depths of the woods, both utterly vanished. The saint's exploits read more like some Norse saga than a Christian chronicle. To protect his humble worshippers, he found himself pursuing an interminable fight with a hideous dragon. Whenever the monster drew blood, the drops which fell to earth at once sprouted lilies of the valley, which still reappear every May, sprinkled throughout the glades and shadows of the forest.

Not only St Leonard's flowers continued to flourish. The dragon must also have produced some offspring, for in the seventeenth century there were tales of another Dragon or Monstrous Serpent which left a glutinous path wherever it dragged itself, and slew anyone who came within range by spitting venom. Several witnesses swore to having seen it, and one man claimed that it had killed mastiffs which he had set on it.

Oddly enough, two centuries after these accounts the fossilised bones of a 25-foot iguanodon were found in St Leonard's Forest south of Crawley. It is tempting to theorise that they had been unearthed all those years earlier and then fearfully covered over again, to provide the germ of a story which swelled ever more terribly with the telling. At all events, such nightmarish fantasies proved very useful to smugglers using the tracks through the forest, and to the occasional robber or highwayman in need of a safe shelter.

North of the forest, sprawling out in all directions over the boundary between West and East Sussex and overflowing both the main London to Brighton road and the London to Brighton railway, close enough to Gatwick airport to catch many of its reverberations, is Crawley.

Once upon a time there was a tidy little town of less than 10,000 souls here. Since the Second World War that figure has been multiplied by seven. A pre-war guidebook brought more or less up to date soon after the war could refer to 'one of the most charming old streets in Sussex, with green ways and trees and delightful houses'. That street is still there, and every attempt was made by the planners of Crawley New

Town to ensure that the character of the old centre should
not be ruined; but the inns have suffered their inevitable fate,
the intelligently husbanded trees cannot help looking a bit
dusty, and one has to accept that there is no way of keeping
just one section of a busy, bustling community for ever in
aspic.

Crawley never attracted admirers the way Rottingdean,
Rye, Shipley or Bosham have always done. The one play-
wright who lived here, Mark Lemon, is remembered not for
his farces and melodramas but for the part he played as
one of the founders and first editor of *Punch*. There is a
window to his memory in the church.

The new town was devised as part of a scheme to take the
load off London after the war. In itself the idea was a sound
one, and as housing and transport within the capital grow
not just steadily worse but uncontrollably worse there are
murmurings about similar projects. For many people, though,
the drawbacks outweigh the advantages. A ring of 'overspill'
towns to attract industry and population out of the congested
city to well-planned towns with the most modern amenities
and with easy access to the countryside sounded appealing at
the start. Crawley was one of the best conceived. Factories
and housing needs were worked out in conjunction with one
another. Shops and schools were well positioned. There was
nothing soulless in it : the relation of each new section to the
attractive older section was carefully worked out. The balance
of trades and professions was calculated so that in no area
would the place be top-heavy. Its large comprehensive school
was not, as are so many of those controversial establishments,
bunged full of children from a mixture of other schools right
from the start, but fed in, as it were, from the bottom with
younger pupils who gradually filled the school up to the top.

All of it a worthy, enlightened concept. One which will,
out of sheer physical necessity, have to be adopted elsewhere
– and very quickly, if we are to survive and ensure the sur-

vival of our countryside and our way of living in and moving about that country. Yet how many of us would not prefer to live in, say, tangled and slightly tatty Horsham, rather than in well-planned Crawley? How long will it be before Crawley looks and *feels* right – right in itself and right for its county?

CHAPTER SIX

The Eastern Weald

The moment we cross the gash of that road from Crawley to Brighton we are offered an embarrassing choice of gardens. It is not that this edge of East Sussex, fertile as it is, has flowered bountifully of its own accord, but that three estates have been fortunate enough to pass through the hands of people with green fingers.

At Handcross, with entrance and exit on an extremely dangerous corner, is Nymans. The well-matched sections of these gardens lead on one from the other, coaxing the visitor not to some culminating rash of colour but to a succession of less flamboyant contrasts. There are a horseshoe-shaped pinetum presenting a dark wall to rolling parkland, judiciously lightened by rhododendrons and azaleas; a laurel walk leading to a sunken garden with cool, shady loggia; a lawn from which it is possible even through the luxuriance of summer foliage to catch a glimpse of distant Chanctonbury; and one of the finest and earliest heather gardens in the country. The pergola carries a great weight of wistaria, and everywhere there are flashes of rhododendron and azalea. Just to add one extravagance of colour in the heart of it all without robbing the more sober trees and shrubs of their special beauty, there is a walled garden with radiant herbaceous borders. The house is still a family home, its southern façade a ruin already romantically overgrown after a fire some years ago.

A short way from Handcross through the woods, best taken at an easy, appreciative pace, are the great beech trees of Balcombe. And beyond, the steep and twisting little road to Ardingly makes a tight arc round Balcombe mill and one of the loveliest corners in Sussex. The lake, the house, the lawn above the water – all too idyllic to be true. The eye is enchanted; the rustle of the valley is a soothing whisper; and there is an indefinable, tangy, meadowsweet smell. It is a lost little world. Soon it may be lost for ever. The whole valley of Southfield Gill and Shell Brook is doomed to become a reservoir. It is hard to decide whether to make a point of visiting it as often as possible before the picture is obliterated, or to dismiss it from the mind now and pretend it never existed.

Crossing the Ouse below Balcombe is the splendid Ardingly viaduct, one of the greatest engineering feats along the railway line to Brighton, still graceful and still visible, unlike the great Brighton viaduct which is now obscured by swarming houses.

At Ardingly is one of the companions to Woodard's college at Lancing. There are also the large permanent showground for the South of England Agricultural Society and, close by, the gardens of Wakehurst Place.

The Wakehurst family to which the estate belonged from Norman times was left in 1454 without a male heir. Two girls, Margaret and Elizabeth, came under the guardianship of Sir John Culpeper. He was not the most efficient or watchful of guardians: the girls were carried off by his own brothers Richard and Nicholas. It was almost obligatory for them to marry after this scandal, whatever the possible unhappiness of such liaisons. In fact one at least of the marriages worked out well, for Nicholas and Elizabeth had ten sons and eight daughters, all shown in Ardingly church on a brass so crowded as to look like a poster warning against rush-hour travel. The other couple had no children.

House and estate were the property of the Culpepers for more than 200 years, until sold off to pay gambling debts. Branches of the Culpeper or Colepeper family were of great importance in both Kent and Sussex. The churches of Ardingly and of Hollingbourne in Kent, near their other great house, seem almost their private domain. Nicholas, the famous herbalist and astrologer, belonged to the branch whose names are to be found in Wilmington and Folkington churches, and who had their own chapel at Robertsbridge.

It is fitting that the old Culpeper estate at Bedgebury in Kent should in 1925 have become the National Pinetum, with one section breeding special trees for Kew, while 40 years later their Wakehurst Place was to be opened as an addition to the Royal Botanic Gardens, Kew. The old herbalist would surely have been happy with such a destiny.

The collecting and nurturing of the trees and shrubs which have shaped the character of the gardens owed a lot to Gerald Loder, later Lord Wakehurst, who bought the estate in 1903, and to Sir Henry Price, who continued the work and bequeathed the results to the National Trust with a generous endowment. The emphasis is arboricultural rather than horticultural, and the gardens are best visited in May, when the rhododendrons are at their finest and the spring foliage brightest, or in autumn to appreciate the cherry, the maple, and a hundred shades of green and gold. Extensive walks through the less formal parts of the grounds include one through impressive rock formations and outcrops of huge, cracked, gnarled roots, themselves like tortured rock. There is a reflective lake in a valley – truly, colourfully reflective – and in late spring the woods themselves appear to rise from another lake, this one of bluebells.

Only someone of exceptional stamina could manage to walk round Wakehurst Place and proceed through Sheffield Park all in one day; but this near neighbour should be visited at the same times of year since it, too, is at its best when the rhododendrons are out or when autumn tints conflict in the mirrors of its five lakes and blur in the ripples below its waterfalls.

The manor belonged to the De La Warr family from the end of the thirteenth century until the middle of the fifteenth, and they returned to it in the eighteenth. In 1769 it was sold to John Baker Holroyd, M.P., who became Baron Sheffield and then Earl of Sheffield. He employed James Wyatt to design him a house, and 'Capability' Brown to landscape the gardens. One of his closest friends was Edward Gibbon, who visited frequently and wrote some chapters of his history while staying here. Gibbon is buried in the Sheffield mausoleum in the church at Fletching – that Fletching where Simon de Montfort encamped the night before his victory at Lewes.

For some years the Australian cricket team opened its Test Match tours of England with a game at Sheffield Park, as the third earl was a keen cricketer and one of the instigators of the whole Test tour idea.

The gardens as we see them today were laid out by Arthur Soames, who bought the estate in 1909, and restored after the Second World War.

One strange phenomenon which many visitors experience from time to time is the anachronistic sound, over the trees, of an engine whistle: the whistle and hiss of a good old-fashioned steam locomotive.

We are near the Bluebell Railway, so called from the spring haze beneath the trees along its five-mile route. Sheffield Park station is its southern terminus and the home of its railway museum. Museum, engines and track are there only because of the determination of a dedicated band of enthusiasts. British Rail closed the line from Lewes to East Grinstead in 1955, but were forced to reopen it the following year after it had been pointed out that, under the terms on which the line had been acquired from the old Southern Railway, such closure was illegal. The stay of execution was only tempo-rary. While obeying the statutory demands to the letter, British Rail contrived to eliminate the most profitable stations on the line and make life as uncomfortable as possible for passengers. In 1958 permission was obtained for final closure.

Precisely one year after this decision, a meeting was held

in Haywards Heath with a view to saving at any rate one stretch of the route. Having decided that it was practicable to maintain a service between Sheffield Park and Horsted Keynes, the preservation society was given three months in which to raise £55,000; which was about all the authorities did give, apart from a generous offer to lease Sheffield Park booking office for five shillings a week. Shaken but unbowed, the Bluebell Railway Preservation Society got the price down to £34,000, and wrangled its way through legal complexities and the demands of safety regulations. Track clearance began, the station was tidied up, and negotiations started for purchase of locomotives and rolling stock before they were broken up for scrap.

Once opened and running regular services, much dependent upon unpaid helpers with week-ends and holidays to spare, the railway proved that there were still thousands of people who regarded it as a pleasure rather than an ordeal to travel in ancient coaches pulled by murky steam locomotives: something like half a million passengers a year. A fund was started for the purchase of historic locomotives, including a 'Terrier' tank engine, the *Fenchurch*, which had done yeoman service on the old London, Brighton and South Coast Railway and at Newhaven docks, and which was treated to an affectionate centenary celebration in 1972. An observation car which had once served for tourist traffic in North Wales was acquired, and the director's saloon of the L.B. & S.C.R. It became possible, and desirable, to employ a number of salaried professional staff to supervise operation and maintenance of the line.

When the lease was due to run out, and British Rail once more tried to sell off the property and put an end to this defiant five miles of permanent way which strove so resolutely to be permanent, more money had to be raised in difficult circumstances, including a governmental 'squeeze' on credit. The fact that the trains are still there, climbing Freshfield

Bank, rumbling over the girder bridge, and wreathing the treetops with swirls of grey and blue smoke, is sufficient evidence of the company's determination.

On 26 August 1973 the *Sunday Times* carried a story about Pickering, in Yorkshire, where some local inhabitants were protesting at the reintroduction of steam trains by a preservation society on their long-abandoned line. A petition was organised, protesting against any return to 'the dirt and smoke associated with steam trains'. Yet the following day *The Times* editorial was recommending that the Minister for Transport Industries 'might usefully dwell on the phenomenon of the flourishing railway preservation societies, and ask himself if there is not a head of steam here that could be harnessed more widely to the public interest'. There are many unprofitable branch lines which might become profitable if operated by local enterprise as a combined tourist attraction and social amenity. Of course such services would have to use a large proportion of diesel engines, and these will never have the same drawing power – in relation to human interest, not to the weight of carriages – as steam. Even the most dedicated advocate of steam engines does not expect them to provide major services again; but there is still enough nostalgia around, and enough interest among the younger generation, to make worth while the preservation of some of the noise and smoke and grit and fun. All through spring, summer and autumn in a dozen Sussex fields, and in heaven knows how many other fields throughout the land, the puff of steam from a traction engine and the jangle of an old steam organ will bring folk from miles around. It is foolish to call the preservationists cranks when they provide so much pleasure.

At the other end of the Bluebell Railway is Horsted Keynes station, some little way from the village itself. Horsted Keynes must always have been a bit baffled to find itself with a railway station at all. Its Tudor cottages, its village green and the shingled spire of its thirteenth-century church have nothing to do with such things. Sheila Kaye-Smith records that one parson, watchful over the tithes due to him, advised his successor : 'Never compound with any parishioner till you have first viewed their land and seen what corn they have upon it'. Their predecessors might have been better advised to claim tithes on the ironstone below rather than the corn above. There were iron workings on all sides here, past Cinder Hill and its lakes, right across Ashdown Forest and ever onwards. West Hoathly, high on the forest ridge to the north-west, has iron grave slabs in the church and hundreds of iron studs in the church door.

The great local iron-masters were the Infields, who built Gravetye Manor. In the late nineteenth century it became the home of the Irish gardener, William Robinson, who introduced the idea of informality and more natural design into landscape gardening, wrote several books on the subject, and founded three weekly gardening magazines. He died here in 1935. Part of the estate is administered by the Forestry Commission, part of it by the hotel into which the manor is now incorporated.

West Hoathly had yet another of the houses where Anne of Cleves could claim to be at home when it suited her; and a fourteenth-century priest's house, itself at one time presented to her, which has been admirably restored and equipped as a museum by the Sussex Archaeological Society. It is best known, though, for its natural formations rather than man's additions. The sandstone of the ridge emerges in great shoulders and humps, poised above gorges eroded along joints in the stone. One especially eccentric balance of boulders is that of Great-upon-Little or Big-on-Little, with the monster on top threatening to roll off its crouching Atlas. The threat seems immediate, but the little rock has been doing its balancing act for untold centuries and the two are unlikely to part company yet.

The old railway line once called at West Hoathly, too, and then crossed a viaduct into East Grinstead; but now its path is the preserve of wild flowers. The most attractive route into the town nowadays takes us past the end of Weir Wood reservoir, with its shaded picnic reservations, and the Victorian grange of Standen on the slopes above.

This house, still a private home, is not in any of the guide-books to historic mansions or architectural gems. Few Victorian piles have yet attained such distinction. But Standen is an interesting piece of work, conceived as it was by an ascetic architect with strong socialist principles at a time when the taste of the new-rich leaned towards over-embellished Gothic. J. S. Beale, a London solicitor, asked Philip Webb to design a family house for week-ends and holidays, with accommodation for visiting friends but no unduly lavish extensions. Webb studied local materials and their use in local building, and came up with this clean-limbed house on its wooded eminence. At one end of the conservatory he allowed himself one of his few little indulgences, a tiny room up a flight of stairs, which he solemnly offered to the youngest daughter of the household on the payment of sixpence. It has ever since been the province of children and their visiting friends.

From this direction one comes quite abruptly into East Grinstead and its wide High Street, with a motley collection of nondescript shop and office frontages on one side and, on the other, a stepped terrace, lined with lime trees, weather-boarding, half-timbering, and a fine stagger of walls and roofs.

Greenstede is Saxon for a green clearing, and the town motto, *Pratis Praesto Viventibus*, proudly confirms that it stands in green meadows. Like Horsham, it was for a time an Assize town: Clarendon House on Judge's Terrace is a survival from those days, when executions took place just outside the judge's lodgings. It was also an iron town, close to that unique mine recorded in Domesday Book, and there are iron milestones at the roadside and iron grave slabs in the church. Buried in the churchyard are three Protestant martyrs burned in June 1556, including a woman, 'patiently abiding what the furious rage of man could say or work against them'.

In 1967 the Adeline Genée Theatre was built, an ambitious venture which has had its ups and downs, and at one stage found itself unwillingly featuring in the national newspapers. Its survival and the scope of its activities must always be problematical in such a relatively small community.

The town's most impressive building is Sackville College, founded in 1609 by the second Earl of Dorset for the shelter of men and unmarried women who had served in his household. These aristocratic almshouses are set around an attractive quadrangle and include a warden's lodging and a chapel. The chapel was rebuilt in 1848, at which time the warden was John Mason Neale, a major translator of material for *Hymns Ancient and Modern* and a contributor in his own right: his works include *Jerusalem the Golden, O Happy Band of Pilgrims*, and *Good King Wenceslas*. Of strong Anglo-Catholic persuasion, he established the sisterhood of St Margaret at Rotherfield in 1854, later moved to East Grinstead.

Buckhurst Park in the parish of Withyham, a short distance from the town, has been a home of the Sackvilles since the time of Henry II. The Thomas Sackville who became first Earl of Dorset was the son of Henry VIII's Chancellor of the Exchequer, and second cousin to Queen Elizabeth I. He had poetic aspirations and began a series of verse moralities about historic Englishmen and the lessons they had learnt in life and in hell; but Court duties commanded too much of his time, and *A Mirror for Magistrates* had to be completed by other hands. Elizabeth made him her Lord High Steward and presented him with Knole in Kent. After her death he served James I as Lord High Treasurer. The family's associations have since been largely with Kent, but their chapel in

Withyham church still houses their banners and memorials, including a recent one to Victoria Sackville-West, the novelist who with her husband, Sir Harold Nicolson, created the gardens of Sissinghurst.

The Buckhurst estate came into the keeping of the De La Warrs, related to the Sackvilles by marriage, and still occupying a more recent house in the park. Of the old building only a tower remains. There used to be a ceremonial salute by a private battery of 14 cannon on family birthdays, the full 14 being reserved for the eldest son's anniversaries. This was abandoned after some of the children, practising for a salute, managed to score a hit on Hartfield High Street.

From the ridge we look south over Ashdown Forest, about which the first thing to be said is that it is not a forest. It is mainly heathland, tufted with copses, thinly garnished with Scots pine, and alternatively soft or bristly underfoot with a variety of mosses and grasses. Cobbett classed it contemptuously with St Leonard's Forest as 'those miserable tracts of heath and fern and bushes and sand'. Parts of it have the mystery, hypnotic to some and hateful to others, of East Anglia's Breckland or a desolate tract of Scotland. The Forestry Commission has done its dismal best to ruin Breckland; the Conservators of Ashdown Forest have done their admirable best to defend their acres.

Standing 800 feet above sea-level, the highest vantage point is Beacon Hill, one of several such in the county. This one is near Crowborough, which Richard Jefferies found so windy and debilitating. The essence of the old hunting forest is concentrated between Forest Row, a mixture of pleasant remains and modern boxes, and Maresfield. Edward II had a hunting lodge at Nutley. Edward III made a gift of the forest to his son John of Gaunt, Duke of Lancaster, which led to its being known for some time as Lancaster Great Park. There are still deer to be found, and still names recalling different activities in the region: Hartfield and Buckhurst speak of the hunt;

Wren's Warren, Crowborough Warren and many other warrens, of the once extensive rabbit population; and Furnace Wood of the industry which annihilated so much of those woods.

In the time of Charles II the forest passed first to the Earl of Bristol and then to the Earls of Dorset, the sixth of whom instituted proceedings for enclosure of certain lands. Very much against his intention, the findings in this case established rights lasting to this day. Although ownership of the land still rests with the De La Warrs, judgment against the sixth Earl of Dorset guaranteed commoners' rights over more than 6,000 acres. This was contested in 1876 by the seventh Earl De La Warr, and after another protracted lawsuit the judge found for the plaintiff. On appeal this decision was reversed, and the parties concerned got together to find a workable compromise. A Board of Conservators was formed to administer the region and ensure the harmonising of different interests. Few today avail themselves of grazing privileges or of the right to cut and carry away wood and bracken, but those rights are still there to be exercised, and in any case the terms under which they were established protect the forest from undesirable encroachments.

During the war there was extensive tank training over the heath, and legislation in 1949 prolonged the right to use it for military purposes. Fortunately no use is made of this right, and we can only hope that it never will be.

This can be breezy country, or it can be ominously still. On a summer's day the valleys and clearings can be sultry, buzzing with insects; or there may be a drifting veil of very fine mist. For the walker there are ancient trackways out of the northern ridge, and for the driver any number of authorised parking and picnic places off the road. Every wanderer has his favourite view, but the best are arguably those between Maresfield and King's Standing, or along the exposed, less-frequented stretch between Wych Cross and King's Standing – the rise from which Edward II watched the hunt being driven up towards him.

Forest Row and Hartfield both in their day had hunting lodges, stables, and accommodation for the king's men. Hartfield church has a charming lych-gate formed by an opening through a pair of sixteenth-century cottages. It also shelters a charming story with a fairy-tale quality. Three hundred years ago a well-to-do eccentric, Nicholas Smith, disguised himself as a beggar and went from village to village finding out who were the generous folk and who the tight-fisted ones. Apparently he had little joy of his fellow men until he reached Hartfield, where he was so well treated that in his will he left enough endowment to ensure that each Good Friday the needy of the parish could receive a bounty.

Farther round the fringe – for there is no settlement of any size within the boundaries of the forest proper – is Crow-borough, a busy town which has lost all real contact with the heaths and woods. Maresfield, on the southern border, would be happier if it were not splintered by an awkward junction of roads where traffic delays build up over hundreds of yards.

Just over a mile to the east, along the under-privileged road where most of these jams occur, is a pub which proudly altered its name some decades ago and now has to do its best to treat the whole thing as a joke.

In 1912 Charles Dawson, a solicitor and keen geologist and antiquarian, announced that he had salvaged fragments of an unusually thick and incredibly ancient human skull from gravel diggings on Pilt Down. With the aid of Sir Arthur Smith-Woodward he dug out other pieces of skull, part of a lower jaw, and a number of primitive flint tools. Anthropologists examining these finds agreed that they could only point to the existence of man much further back in prehistory that had ever been thought possible. The popular phrase 'missing link', postulating a transitional stage between ape and human, was much bandied about. The creature was named *Eoanthropus Dawsoni* after its discoverer, and in 1938 a memorial to Dawson was erected on the site.

Not all experts were entirely happy about the authenticity of Piltdown Man. In 1953 and 1954, intensive investigation with modern techniques such as fluorine and radioactivity tests showed that the jawbone was certainly non-human and was probably that of a young orang-outan, and that although the cranium was human it had been artificially stained with sulphate of iron to falsify its age and match the soil conditions in which it was found. Other items had been treated in the same way, and on one there were the marks of cutting with a modern knife.

The memorial to Dawson still stands and the pub still trades under the sign of the *Piltdown Man*. In spite of much theorising, nobody is sure who perpetrated the complicated fraud or why it was done; though one needs no carbon dating or pigment tests to strengthen the suspicion that Charles Dawson himself could hardly have been entirely innocent.

Uckfield is a hilly thoroughfare town with little to delay the traveller. In the church are the gravestone and trim little brass of John Fuller, gentleman and iron-master, ancestor of a far more remarkable John Fuller who is waiting for us in Brightling. Neighbouring Framfield has a brass to the Gage family, and a churchyard which is more like a formal garden.

Some way towards Lewes, near Halland, are the Bentley Wildfowl Gardens. This private collection was begun in 1962 and now offers to the public on certain days between April and September a display of wildfowl including cranes, swans, geese, flamingoes and peacocks.

For all the sterility of its sandy soils, Ashdown Forest is the birthplace of three beneficent rivers: the Medway (which defects to Kent as soon as it can manage it), the Ouse and the eastern Rother. Here I must declare what I refuse to call a prejudice, since it arises from experience rather than pre-judgment, and is a bias only in the sense that I now fully

recognise my own leanings and see no good reason for denying them. To me, then, the course of the Rother from source
to sea is the most enchanting and enchanted of all the highways, by-ways and waterways of south-eastern England.

Mark Antony Lower, without whose informative ghost no
right-minded explorer sets off across this part of the world,
asserted that the infant Rother 'rises in the cellar of the
mansion called Rother House in the parish of Rotherfield'.
From there it ambles through its blissful childhood in the
Weald and, in adolescence, flirts with some of the prettiest
girls in Kent; but keeps them firmly in their place and asserts
its maturity by abandoning an old relationship with New
Romney in favour of the charms of Rye.

Rotherfield is small but its church is large. It has an imposing shingled spire above a shingled roof, and a Burne-Jones
window. The pulpit is a turmoil of lions and vultures, and the
font cover has some graphically carved panels. There must
once have been a near-continuous picture gallery of wall
paintings, of which a few scenes have been liberated from
Cromwellian whitewash. The church is dedicated to St Denys,
following the original building offered by a Saxon chief in
thanksgiving for a miraculous cure effected in a French
monastery.

The Rother sidles round below Mayfield, through rich
farm lands which were once rich iron workings. There are
remains of old watermills, millponds, and the wagon ponds
into which, after hot iron hoops had been hammered on to
their wheels, wagons were driven to cool and contract the
metal. And it is not impossible to find the occasional heated
swimming pool.

St Dunstan is said to have founded a church in Mayfield in
Saxon times, though the present one belongs only to the
fifteenth century. When his original building was completed
it proved to be askew, but Dunstan put that right with one
thrust of his shoulder. It is also recounted that he had an

unwelcome visitor while he was engaged in his craft of iron working – an odd legend, in view of the Saxon neglect of these resources and of his monastic calling. However that may be, this visitor came in the semblance of a beautiful girl, but revealed cloven hoofs to the saint's keen gaze. Dunstan lunged with his red-hot tongs and pinched the guest's nose. Forsaking his disguise, the devil howled and ran away to plunge his nose into a stream which has since been known for its sulphurous taste.

Tongdean Farm on the Downs is supposed to have been named after some such episode, but Dunstan would scarcely have hurled his tongs such a distance; and the nearness of the farm to the Devil's Dyke suggests that romantic tale spinners have muddled their myths. In any case, the tongs were lodged for many years in the Mayfield Convent of the Holy Child, established in the nineteenth century on the ruins of a palace once used by the archbishops of Canterbury.

The village sign shows, in addition to St Dunstan, girls dancing in a field, to support the derivation of Mayfield from Maids' Field. Red roofs along the main street flush most deeply at sunset, and sixteenth-century, half-timbered Middle House has become a warming, welcoming inn.

Fields are as common as dens and hursts hereabouts. Descending to the south, climbing and descending again according to the vagaries of which winding road we choose, we are soon in Heathfield. Old Heathfield is more satisfying than the new. Its adjoining hamlet of Cade Street has a memorial plaque to Jack Cade, leader of the Kentish rising of 1450. With Sussex and Kentish rebels he defeated royal troops at Sevenoaks and marched on London in protest against unreasonable taxation and general misgovernment. When his followers disbanded after being given the vaguest of promises, he was hunted down and killed by Alexander Iden, a Kentish yeoman. There is some dispute as to whether this death really occurred here or at Hothfield in Kent; and it is pointed out that Cade Street is only a corruption of the earlier Cart Street.

One monument which cannot be argued away is that in Heathfield Park. Here, restored and opened to the public in 1973, is the Gibraltar Tower.

During the Seven Years' War and the tussle for supremacy in the Caribbean, Britain captured Havana. Second-in-command at the engagement was General Sir George Eliott, who used his prize money to buy the estate of Heathfield Park. Under cover of the American War of Independence France tried to regain some of what she considered her rightful possessions, and Spain came into the war on the promise of having Gibraltar, among other places, restored. Sir George Eliott was in command of the Rock when siege was laid to it in 1779, and with a courageous garrison maintained unfaltering resistance through the most dreadful privations until relieved by Admiral Howe in 1783. The Peace of Versailles in September of that year confirmed, as Eliott had already personally done, British control of Gibraltar.

Sir George was raised to the peerage as Lord Heathfield, Baron of Gibraltar. In the few years remaining to him he was able to spend little time in his seventeenth-century mansion, and died in Aix-la-Chapelle in 1790. He was brought home for burial in the parish church. The brass plate of his monument is a souvenir from a floating battery captured from the Spanish.

In 1792 Sir Francis Newbury, who had bought the estate, decided to assemble other souvenirs in a worthy setting. He built a 55-foot tower and installed in it a display of Lord Heathfield's personal belongings, including some which had been with him on Gibraltar, a desk, and his sword. At some stage the collection was dispersed. The last reference to the sword was in 1909, when an American bought it from a local farm labourer and presumably carried it home with him. The Gibraltar Tower was neglected, and during the Second World

War its spiral staircase and floors were burnt out by a fire carelessly lit by a soldier on duty there. After the war its upper masonry began to crumble and fall in.

Dr Gerald Moore and his wife bought the estate in 1968, and set about an ambitious scheme not merely of restoration but of developing all the resources of the park. The tower was carefully renovated, following as closely as possible the original design and materials. A collection of military effects was begun, to form the basis of a small museum in the setting envisaged by Sir Francis Newbury. The exhibits are related as closely as possible to regiments linked with Lord Heathfield's career, but where material adding to a more general background picture has become available, it has been incorporated. There are several magnificent helmets, including one of the Fifth Dragoon Guards worn during the charge of the Heavy Brigade at the battle of Balaclava.

Outside, there are landscaped gardens, setting off three bronze figures by Dr Moore. He has also laid out a wild-life park, a small motor museum whose star piece is Rudyard Kipling's last Rolls-Royce, and the beginnings of a collection of Victoriana in the old Royal Box acquired from Sandown Park. All this was opened to the public at Easter 1973, and will be open annually between Easter and the end of October.

A couple of miles south of Heathfield is a village which until just before the Second World War appeared on the map as Horeham Road. The linguistically unarguable identification of the place as a Whore's Home distressed local inhabitants so much that the name was prissily watered down to Horam.

Nothing is watered down, and nothing artificially fortified, in the establishment which today dominates the main road through the village.

In the days when I worked for a while in a large international company, and when 'Merrydown Cider' was making a name for itself, one impish executive enjoyed startling his more sedate colleagues at solemn conferences by saying, 'Oh, yes, I know one of the chaps who started that – we were in prison together'. He would protract the joke for as long as possible before revealing that he meant a prisoner-of-war camp.

The chaps who started the business were Jack Ward and Ian Howie, who in 1946 set about proving in a house called Merrydown, in Rotherfield, that 'the grape was not the only fruit capable of yielding a palatable fermented beverage'. Every grandmother throughout the country had her own recipe, mellow or lethal, for parsnip or rhubarb wine; but Ward and Howie aimed at establishing a consistent quality and producing in commercial quantities. After the war they formed a company which in its first year made 450 gallons of what they designated vintage cider, and 400 gallons of redcurrant wine. They were forced to take part-time jobs elsewhere while they built up the business – buying second-hand bottles, doing all their own bottle-washing and filling by hand – but by 1947 were expanding healthily enough to need more spacious premises. This was when they moved into Horam Manor, a seventeenth-century house at one time the home of the ancestors of Lady Hart-Dyke, latterly used as a hotel and gutted by fire early in the war.

In rebuilding, a subterranean passage was revealed, and during extensions early in 1973 a second came to light. These inevitably gave rise to stories about smugglers, and the place is undoubtedly close enough to Pevensey Levels to have provided a useful storage and distribution centre for the 'free traders'. Today the winery is more respectable, and the edicts of the Customs and Excise are scrupulously observed, even when they may lead, as once they nearly did, to financial ruin.

In 1955 Merrydown's output had reached 300,000 gallons a year. The government then adjusted concessions hitherto protecting domestic industries and slapped a crippling duty on cider of 15° proof. This meant the company had to raise its price by 50 per cent, causing a two-thirds drop in sales. It took ten years to fight back to the 1955 level. But there was no skimping and no lowering of standards: instead, alcohol content was raised, and it was decided to change the name of vintage cider to the apter one of apple wine.

All the apples used in the process come from Kent and Sussex. Each ton provides 180 gallons for an 18-month cycle before the finished product reaches the customer. Additions to the range over recent years include gooseberry, elderberry, white currant, and even a sparkling strawberry wine. And, reviving a traditional Anglo-Saxon tipple, mead has become a best-seller and is exported in large quantities to many countries, including Australia, the United States, and Holland.

Orthodox medical practitioners tend to scorn the therapeutic value of cider vinegar, attributing any cures of rheumatic patients to a sort of faith healing. But agricultural cider vinegar is sold in bulk to farmers, to keep cattle generally fit and to help combat mastitis – 'And farmers', observes Ray Springett of Merrydown, 'are the last people to pay out good money for something that doesn't work'. These and other non-alcoholic products are marketed under the trade name Martlet, after the six heraldic birds of the county arms.

It is a really local, really Sussex industry; and, in spite of that early side-swipe at the snob cult of the grape, it is playing its part in re-establishing the viniculture which the Romans brought to southern England. Merrydown provides facilities for vineyards too small to operate pressing and bottling plant of their own, or blends some of their output into a white wine labelled Anderida. From its own vineyard it produces a riesling sylvaner from Mueller Thurgau cuttings, and experiments with grafting European vine varieties on to American rootstocks. New cultivars produced by Continental researchers have been planted for observation. Quality so far is excellent, but quantities unreliable: in one recent year, the vagaries of an English summer reduced output to a few dozen bottles.

Visitors come by the coach-load, and although they are made welcome it has become necessary to arrange bookings well in advance. A pleasant adjunct to such a visit, though unconnected with Merrydown, is a nature trail starting from the adjacent car park.

Another memorial we might have noted while in Heathfield was that to the Lewes martyrs of the Marian persecution. They are lumped together because of their execution at one place, but were of various origins. The most imposing figure was that of Richard Woodman, a man of some learning and of considerable standing in the neighbourhood of Warbleton, east of the road between Heathfield and Horam. An ironmaster employing a hundred men, he was accustomed to speak his mind, and as churchwarden of St Mary's did so most vigorously when his rector chose to turn 'head to tail and preach clean contrary to that which he had before taught', as Foxe puts it in the *Book of Martyrs*. Woodman's public accusation that the priest had before-time taught them one thing and now was preaching another led to his arrest and confinement in prison, where he remained a year and a half without trial but subject to frequent verbal examination. Then, unexpectedly, he was freed.

Soon his voice was raised again. Word had spread that his release was due to his having recanted his beliefs, and this he would not allow: he stumped from parish to parish denying such rumours and expressing his real views so vehemently that his arrest was again ordered. The men who came to take him away had forgotten to bring the warrant, which gave Woodman a wonderful opportunity for one of his harangues, warning them, 'if you come in my house before you have it, at your own adventure'. All three went away, probably thankful to escape the last of his tongue for a while, and asked the Constable to post men so that the heretic should not escape. Before the guard could be set, however, Woodman had fled his house.

It was rumoured that he had got away to Flanders. In fact he hid for six or seven weeks in the woods, to which his wife brought food every day, and where he had plenty of time to continue reading his Bible. Once it was thought that he was out of the country, vigilance at the ports slackened, and he decided it would now be wise actually to leave England. But he was not a man to skulk abroad. Longing for his wife and children, he returned and hid in his own home, doing such work as he could and dodging visitations by his enemies, as many as 20 at a time searching the house and each time going away empty-handed.

Finally he was betrayed – by his own father and brother, he believed – and in a surprise raid the searchers came close to the hiding-place he had fitted up for himself. He broke his way out and made a run for it, but had been given no time to put his shoes on, so that his feet were cut about by sharp cinders in the lane. A particularly jagged one brought him down, and he was seized.

> Then they tooke me and led me home agayne
> to put on my shoes and such gere as I had
> neede of. Then sayd John Fauconer; 'Now
> your master hath deceaved you. You said
> you were an Angell, why did you not fly
> away from us?' 'Then' said I, 'what be
> they that ever heard me say that I was an
> Angell? It is not the first lye by a
> thousand that they have made of me.
> Angells were never begotten of men, nor
> borne of women; but if they had said, that
> they had heard me say, that I do trust I
> am a saint, they had not said amysse. 'What?
> doo you thinke to be a saint?' 'Yea that I
> doo, and am already, in Gods sight. I trust
> in God; for he that is not a saint in Gods

sight already is a devill. Therefore he
that thinketh scorne to be a sainte, let him
be a devill.'

Assertions of this kind were unlikely to endear him to his
accusers. Nevertheless there was for some time a possibility
that he might once again be spared. The Bishop of Chichester,
charged with his interrogation, enjoyed their disputations,
respected Woodman's viewpoint, and invited him to dinner.
But in the end the pressures were too great and Woodman too
intransigent. When the Bishop of Winchester finally pronounced sentence on 'the naughtiest verlet hereticke that
ever I knew', the condemned man still had the spirit to reply,
'if you condemn me, you will be damned, if you repent it not'.
The cinder lane along which he fled can still be walked,
preferably with shoes on, half a mile north of the village,
turning towards Heathfield.
Warbleton church is set high on its mound, overlooking a
steep hill and the local inn, which has long had its punning
sign of 'War-bill-in-Tun', showing a halberd thrust into a tun
of ale. More tolerant than Woodman's inquisitors, Sir John
Lade of Warbleton, who died in 1740 and has an impressive
marble monument within the church, loyally supported the
Crown and the Established Church but is praised as having
been 'without acrimony to dissenters'. His tolerance had some
limits, though, for it is also noted that he 'as a true Englishman despised all for what he thought the good of his
Country'.
Overweening pride on the part of the local squire must
have been fostered by the loftiness of the mighty manorial
pew: reached by 12 steps, it could not fail to make a man
feel monarch of all he surveyed.
There is a fine large fifteenth-century brass to William
Prestwyck, rector of the parish and at one time dean of St
Mary's College, Hastings. A pelican in piety feeds its young

217

on the pinnacle of the canopy. This bird might seem indigenous to these parts. Three pelicans appear in the arms of the Pelhams, lavishly displayed all over the county: here impaling Lewknor in the north window of the chancel. A few miles away in East Hoathly the Pelham buckle appears in the dripstones of the tower doorway, and even closer, at Dallington, the tower has its pelicans and buckle.

The buckle in the device is a battle honour which became the lasting pride of the Pelhams. When King John of France was defeated at Poitiers in 1365, he surrendered his sword to two Sussex knights, Sir Roger de la Warr and Sir John de Pelham. Sir Roger added the crampet, or scabbard end-plate, to his arms, and Sir John the sword-belt buckle. Wherever the Pelhams had influence, pelicans and buckle appeared: on their seal, in ironwork, in the masonry of their homes, on church towers and in church windows.

It was this Sir John's son, another Sir John, who supported Bolingbroke on his way to becoming Henry IV, while his wife defended Pevensey. A third John was chamberlain of the household to Henry V's French wife, who in due course granted him administration of her widespread properties. By judicious intermarriage with other leading families, and by skilful avoidance of peerages and other honours which might embroil them in envious and probably fatal squabbles, the Pelhams managed to survive many centuries without any serious disruption. Sir Nicholas Pelham remained unscathed and widely respected through all the shifts and swings of fortune between the days of Henry VIII and those of Elizabeth I. He is best remembered for his rallying of friends and local yeomen to fight off a surprise French attack on Seaford, with the result that, according to his monument in Lewes, 'This Pelham did repel 'em back aboard'.

An eighteenth-century member of the family merits less admiration. Henry Pelham became Secretary for War in 1724, Paymaster of the Forces, and, in 1743, First Lord of the

Treasury. He was a great friend and supporter of Robert Walpole, and his methods, like Walpole's, rested upon systematic and unblenching corruption.

In 1801 Thomas Pelham, a rather more conscientious M.P., was created first Earl of Chichester, and under that title the Pelham line continues in the ninth earl of today.

For all their unmistakable emblem upon Dallington's tower, the Pelhams surely take second place in that village and its environs to Squire John Fuller, who has left some of his own odd devices upon the landscape. Like Richard Woodman an iron-master, and like Richard Woodman outspoken, he lived in an age when it was no heresy to speak one's mind, though it might not always be politic. From his forthrightness and the impulsive outburst of his enthusiasms he was known by some as Honest Jack Fuller, by others as Mad Jack Fuller.

Born in 1756, he was one of the last to make a tidy fortune out of the iron industry, and also inherited money from estates in Jamaica. Some of his money he put into electioneering, and became M.P. for Lewes, being known in Parliament as the Hippopotamus because of his girth. It must have taken some strength to shift him on the occasion when he had to be bodily ejected from the House after a filibuster ending in his insulting the Speaker. At one juncture he was offered a peerage, but declared, 'I was born Jack Fuller, and Jack Fuller I'll die.'

He was rumbustious and argumentative, but also had an inquiring, scientific mind. He was generous with his time, with the encouragement he gave to talent when he recognised it, and with money for the needy. The young Turner owed a lot to him. He saved Bodiam castle from complete destruction, and in time of depression provided employment by having a wall built around his large estate.

The estate was originally called Rose Hill, later Brightling Park. In it he set up a domed observatory, and on a hilltop placed Brightling Needle, an obelisk which is a welcome friend to the returning native and a great help to the stranger seeking a landmark. One of his more notable follies is the 'Sugar Loaf' at Wood's Corner, just above Dallington. Having bet a friend that the church's stone spire was visible from his house, he went home to find that it wasn't; so, having duly paid his debt, he constructed this dunce's hat in such a place that it could, from his windows, be mistaken for the spire.

Jack Fuller died in 1834. His grave in Brightling church-yard is marked by a high pyramid within which his corpse was said, with little foundation other than the wish to believe him eccentric to the last, to have been installed in evening dress at a dinner-table, with a bottle in his hand.

His pseudo-spire at Wood's Corner was used as a cottage until 1880, at one stage occupied by a hermit who may well have been as eccentric as Jack himself. In 1961 it was repaired by public subscription and given into the keeping of the county council.

The ridgeways look down on either side into valleys whose floors are almost invisible between a velvety carpet of trees, with here and there the flicker of red tiles, a patch of white plaster, or the darker, unsprouting timber of a barn. The forests seem to be summoning up their strength to win back their old terrain. They might meet stiff opposition on the crests, where modern roads and more substantial settlements are firmly planted; but in the valley, sub-divided by their own patterns of ridge, vale and hummock, the roads are tortuous and unconfident, and could easily be conquered.

South-east of Dallington, no map and no well-meaning directions will really help the stranger. He must make his own way, enjoying every wrong turning and every unex-pected plunge of the lanes. If he perseveres, he will find . . . well, what *will* he find? Simply that he is lost – lost in a timeless world where the past, even with cars just audible along the high road, and a tractor humping itself up a slope, is more real than the present. Even more: there is no real past, no real present. Each time I go towards Ashburnham and Penhurst, I feel that I may never emerge again; that there is nowhere outside to which one could emerge anyway, no outside whatsoever.

In St Peter's church, 44 members of the Ashburnham family lie in their wide vault. There were Ashburnhams here for more than 300 years, since the rebuilding and reconsecration of the church in the seventeenth century. But even before that we have records of them: in 1156 Reginald de Oseburnham was making grants of land to Robertsbridge Abbey, an Ashburnham fought at Crécy, an Ashburnham who fell foul of Elizabeth 1 lost the estates to the queen's cook, but his son regained them.

One John Ashburnham – there were many of this name – remained loyal to Charles 1 until the end, and by the king's wish was presented with certain relics after the execution. As the January day was bitterly cold, Charles put on two shirts so that he might not appear to be shivering with fear. One of these, together with a pair of silk drawers, a pair of garters, a watch, and a monogrammed sheet which had been thrown over the body, came to Ashburnham. The relics were kept for many years in the church, so that sufferers from scrofula might still attempt a cure of this 'King's Evil' by a vicarious touch. In 1830 the church was broken into, and the case of the watch was among items stolen. The remainder were taken into safe keeping at Ashburnham Place.

The iron railings in the church probably came from Ashburnham Forge, the last of all the Wealden furnaces to blow. Its hammer ponds are dry now but their contours can still be identified, and the occasional cannon-ball still turns up from a ploughed surface or out of the undergrowth. Near-by is Cinder Hill Farm.

On the tower doorway of the church are the Pelham

buckles, and their arms are flaunted again in a window at Penhurst.

The church at Penhurst has a decrepit but still notable fifteenth-century timber porch, an oak screen of the same period, and a carved oak pulpit thought to have been brought here from Long Melford in Suffolk. Mounting the steps of this pulpit the pastor is faced, before turning to his congregation, with admonitory white lettering on a black plaque: 'Sir, we would see Jesus'.

No more delightful neighbour could be imagined for the church than the Elizabethan manor house, built of the same Wealden sandstone. The last survivor of the Ashburnham iron workers, who died in 1883, once described to the rector the last job they undertook: the casting of three fire-backs for this house, where they are still in regular use.

Turning back towards the Dallington–Netherfield road, the traveller is beckoned on by Mad Jack's Observatory, the Needle, and Brightling itself. Who would not gladly drink to the immortal, impudent memory in the *Fullers Arms*?

There is an unexpected flutter of industry in one corner here. In Limekiln Wood near Netherfield, above the reservoir, is a gypsum mine, unobtrusive despite its overhead cableway. The gypsum deposits were discovered by accident in the 1870s, when trial borings were sunk in a scientific inquiry into local rock formations. The investigators did not discover what they were looking for, but found instead this rich source of plaster. Mines were soon working, and are still working; more deposits have been located and opened up, without any intolerably harmful effect on the landscape.

*   *   *

On a number of corners stand posts pointing towards Bateman's, and down from the ridge we should go, over the little River Dudwell, to turn along the lane at the end of which the spacious Jacobean stone house waits behind its yew hedge.

Yet again we are on iron-founders' territory. The Nether Forge (nether in respect to Burwash) worked beside the stream here until the industry declined, and the fortunes of its masters with it. Bateman's became a farmhouse and then was abandoned. It was put to rights towards the end of the last century and rediscovered in 1902 by Rudyard Kipling, who, in flight from the autograph hunters of Rottingdean, found the peace he was seeking from the brash present, without menace from a sombre past: 'We went through every room and found no shadow of ancient regrets, stifled miseries, nor any menace, though the "new" end of her was three hundred years old'. He and his wife installed their own electrical generating plant, harnessing the Dudwell just as it had once been harnessed for bellows and hammers. They bought more adjoining property and set to work on the gardens, the hedges, and the pond.

Like many another immigrant, Kipling had already fallen in love with the county, and at Bateman's that love blossomed. Other parts of Britain have captivated newcomers and in many cases held them for a lifetime; but few can have prompted such paeans of adoration as Sussex. Cowper and Blake both thought it close to heaven itself. Coventry Patmore's cherished ambition, realised at last, was to settle in Hastings. Two Americans, Henry James and Conrad Aiken, both chose Rye. Hilaire Belloc, French by birth, came under the spell. Kipling, born in India, rejoiced that out of all possibilities Sussex by the sea should prove 'beloved over all'. There is sentimentality in many of the sentiments; but the magic, whatever it may be, is powerful and not to be too brashly derided.

A hill beyond the garden became Pook's Hill, setting for a pageant of English history as Kipling saw it. He continued to travel about the world, but temperamentally sank more and more deeply into Sussex, until his death in 1936. A gate of wrought iron leading from the walled garden preserves the initials R.K., and many of the rooms in Bateman's are fitted out as they were during his working life.

On the ridge north of the house is Burwash, a long street with a file of pollarded limes, the unforgettable *Bell Inn*, and a wavering line of houses and cottages with hardly a dull or depressing face among them. Noblest of them all is Rampyndene, close to the church.

The iron gates of St Barnabas's porch were locally made, and the oldest known Sussex iron grave slab, from Socknersh, is in the churchyard. Within the church is another Pelham buckle, this time on the font.

We can no more escape talking about iron hereabouts than we could escape talking about coal in the Rhondda valley. There were forges between here and Mayfield, between here and Wadhurst, between here and Ticehurst; and behind us, as we have seen, all the way over Brightling and Dallington and Warbleton.

Wadhurst's village sign portrays an anvil, a tree, and oasthouses. The hop-gardens are comparatively new, shared with Kent across the border. The tree is rightly symbolic: all the timber used in the restoration of Westminster Hall roof came from the Whiligh estate just outside Wadhurst. As for the anvil, one glance inside the church will supply the answer. Its floor is dark with memorial slabs, 33 in all, cast with the names of the local iron-founding families. Dividing the bell-ringing chamber from the nave is a modern glass and welded steel screen, 17 feet high, donated by the descendant of a family of blacksmiths in memory of his ancestors and of the Sussex iron industry. Motifs in the screen show the produce of the Sussex countryside, and those on the side slips – oak leaf and blacksmith's hammer, anvil and pincers – recall the wood and iron of the furnaces and forges. (It was not until I came to work on this book that I learned from a casual remark, to my great gratification, that my own uncle made the moulds for these reliefs down the slips). The whole is surmounted by frisky Sussex lambs, six Sussex martlets, and the hop. The lambs are, candidly, rather twee; but then, skipping lambs tend to be twee.

Between 1960 and 1968 excavations were carried out at Bardown, outside Wadhurst, to study the layout of a Romano–British site to which attention had been drawn by the existence of a dump of ancient refuse, largely iron slag. During the hundred years of its operation, this settlement is thought to have produced at least 10,000 tons of iron, and there was also some tile and pottery making. The tiles are significant, being stamped CL BR, which suggests that the site came under the authority of *Classis Britannica*, the Roman fleet. Wadhurst is some distance from the sea but not impossibly far from the Rother or Medway, and accessible along the ridgeway above the Wild. The community's probable function was to supply material for distribution by military supply ships to coastal garrisons and those in the turbulent north, along with the products of similar workings near Battle and Crowhurst.

Dedicated to present leisure rather than past industry, Wadhurst Park was recently opened as a recreational centre for sailing, riding, fishing and grass ski-ing. There is also a small animal and bird reserve.

Straddling the county border, with its newer house in Kent and the old monastery ruins on a lovely turn of the little River Teise in Sussex, is the estate of Bayham Abbey. The abbey was founded early in the thirteenth century by monks from two Premonstratensian communities, the White Canons of Otham in Sussex and of Brockley in Kent. There was obvious rivalry between different monastic orders over territorial demarcations, since an agreement had to be drawn up between the White Canons here and the Austin Canons of Salehurst Abbey, near Robertsbridge, stipulating that neither should erect any place, cell or abbey within four leagues of the other's house. In 1229 Bayham and the Austin prior of

Michelham quarrelled over the jurisdiction of a chapel at Hailsham, and kept up the dispute for ten years.

The main patrons of Bayham were the Sackvilles. St Richard of Chichester, himself an admirer of the Dominican order of Black Friars, enjoyed visiting this abbey of the White Friars, and the bed in which he slept was one of the many of his relics thought to have miraculous properties.

In 1525 Wolsey dissolved the monastery, but it suffered less physical damage in succeeding years than many similar foundations. Today there remain fair sections of the gate-house, sacristy and chapter house, some segments around the cloister, and parts of the elaborate church with its lofty central crossing. The root tentacles of a leaning, windswept tree bid fair either to tear out the stones of one wall or to crush the whole wall into the ground.

Dodging past Lamberhurst, we contrive to stay in Sussex and come to Ticehurst, no picture-book village but a bright, hospitable place for all that. Its parish church does not shut itself away from its people: one grassy edge of the church-yard opens straight on to a lane without even a fence, facing an amiable row of tiled and timbered houses, set off by a riot of flowers in spring and summer. In the churchyard Mary Baker, a domestic in the family of the Earl of Dorset, decided in 1797 to stake her claim to a desirable patch of land by erecting a tombstone with the inscription: 'Mary Baker intends to lie here'.

It is most appropriate that many great stones of the church and its heavy tower should, in this ironstone corner of the country, be smeared with wide trickles of rusty discolo-ration.

On a brass within the chancel is a tall knight flanked by two deferential ladies whose heads are on a level with his hips. The man was Sir John Wybarne, who died in 1490; his companions 'Edith and Agnes his true wives' – true one at a time, presumably.

Across the rivers Limden and Rother is Etchingham, whose church boasts six brasses. The oldest, lacking a head, is of Sir William de Echyngham, who died in 1388 shortly after completing the church about the remains of an earlier Norman building. There are heraldic shields and windows, and some lovingly executed misericords in the choir.

Robertsbridge is not, as might at first appear, a bridge over the Rother – there is in fact more than one bridge over the river – but quite literally Robert's bridge, the man in question being the Robert de Sancto Martino who is credited with the foundation of the Cistercian abbey here. After the Dissolution the abbey and some of its lands were presented by Henry VIII to Sir William Sidney, father of Sir Philip Sidney. Sir William at once set up in the most characteristic local business by adapting the building to take a furnace and forges, and housing his workers in vacant rooms.

This addition to the batteries of furnaces already gobbling up wood produced a strong protest from Hastings, Rye and Winchelsea. It was not that the freemen of these Cinque Ports were enlightened conservationists: they worried only that the sources of their profitable timber exports were not merely drying up but being burnt up. A royal commission of inquiry was called for, but before its findings had been promulgated a large band of demonstrators arrived with the intention of smashing up the forges. The abbey escaped destruction, however, and continued making iron and casting cannon until 1801, using the Rother to transport its products all year round. Then, like the abbey itself, the furnace and forges decayed, and in the end the whole jumble was incorporated into a farm.

The main London to Hastings road is both too busy and too narrow for the village. To widen it would be unthinkable, with so many pleasant buildings gracing that slope. But the alternative is for them all to be shaken to dust. Nobody is going to bother with a by-pass, for Robertsbridge is of no consequence to the planners, and not strong or wealthy enough to give orders to such planners. Although larger than many a spire-crowned hamlet we have been through in our travels, it does not even have its own church, but shares the one on the hill of Salehurst.

Here there is a peculiar circlet of salamanders around the font. And here the arms of the Echynghams and Culpepers. And somewhere in the vicinity, in what would have been the abbey or one of its chapels, must lie the bodies of Sir Edward Dalyngruge, builder of Bodiam castle, and the Sir John Pelham who won the buckle for his descendants' gratification.

*   *   *

Riding home from Robertsbridge to Rye one dark night towards the end of the seventeenth century, Samuel Jeake the younger very nearly came off his horse in the mire. The animal stumbled through a runnel of water, and the saddle slid forward over its ears. Jeake, a severe Puritan who sought God's specific guidance on every little detail of his life, did so now. The Lord directed him, he later recalled, 'to retire at once' before being thrown forward over his horse's head, and, with thanks for this divine inspiration, he pulled himself back. In addition to being a Puritan, Jeake somehow contrived to be simultaneously a great believer in the influence of the stars. The moment he was safely home he cast his horoscope, finding without surprise that it showed water to be in the ascendant.

I, too, am about to travel home to Rye, but not on horseback and not over such treacherously rutted roads. In any case, I am not one to lose my footing here. On these remaining acres of Sussex beyond the Hastings to Hawkhurst highway, within the embrace of the Kent ditch, I hold, if not the freehold, at any rate a lifetime's lease of incalculable worth.

Any parent will confirm that the eating habits of children fall into two main categories, which may well be an indication of their temperament throughout life. There are those who gobble down the choicest delicacies right away; and those who save the best until the end. I confess to being a saver. I have kept the best for the end, and, given author's licence, propose now to make quite a meal of it.

CHAPTER SEVEN

To the Kent Ditch

'God save Englonde and the Towne of Rye'. So prayed the Rye Customal as written down in 1564, based on practices which had existed a long time before that; so long, indeed, that the preamble asserted:

These byn the usages of the Comynalty
of the Towne of Rye used there of tyme
out of mynde whiche mens myndes cannot
think to the contrary.

Rye's sense of its independence could not be better exemplified than in that appeal to save England *and* the town. It was for centuries one of the bulwarks of England, but wished to make clear that it was so on its own terms. Never under the sway of a great lord, the town was always one of craftsmen, sailors and merchants, all fairly well convinced that every man should aspire to be a freeman, and jealous of their Cinque Port privileges.

Its very appearance is defiant. The sandstone hill rises straight out of the narrow coastal plain, simply asking to be fortified. Those red roofs, narrow streets and closely packed houses, crowned by the little cap of the great church, might be accused today of winsomeness – 'so quaint', you will hear the voices as the cameras click and whirr – but if you search you will still find remains of that tough encircling wall which belted the townsfolk in and kept their enemies out; and there is still one of the sturdy gateways through that wall.

The manor of Rameslege or Rameslie, covering a stretch of seaboard between Hastings and Rye, was promised to the abbey of Fécamp by the exiled Ethelred the Unready if ever he was restored to his throne. Once that restoration had been accomplished, he forgot his promise, and it was left to his widow to persuade her new husband, Canute, to honour it. William the Conqueror confirmed Fécamp's jurisdiction over the region, and when punishing surrounding districts for their part in opposing his landing he did no damage to Rameslie or its fishing village of La Rie or Rhie, a name deriving perhaps from the French *rie*, a bank of the sea, or Old English 'at the island'.

When William's successors fought to hold their French possessions, Rye was in the forefront of the battle. In 1339 a fleet of more than 60 French ships attacked the town, burning 52 houses and a windmill; whereupon an English fleet gave chase and, in return, sacked Boulogne. In the dreadful year 1377, whose devastations at Hastings and Rottingdean we have already noted, the French succeeded in occupying Rye and using it as a stronghold from which to despoil the surrounding countryside. The abbot of Battle gathered men around him and set up headquarters in Winchelsea, which scared the intruders away, but not before they had helped themselves to a massive cargo of valuables, including the church bells, and set fire to the town. A return match was played the following year. Combined forces from Rye and Winchelsea raided the Normandy coast, ransacked churches and smashed down houses, set fire to Dieppe, and recovered the bells of Rye.

The Cinque Ports were not invariably inhospitable to foreigners. Huguenot refugees had been steadily trickling into the country before 1572, and after the massacre of St Bartholomew's Eve the number in Rye alone soon amounted to 1,500. Small as the town was, it welcomed them as reinforcements for a population devastated by plague. After the Revocation of the Edict of Nantes in 1685 there was another influx. French and Flemish influences would undoubtedly have affected the style and construction of the Tudor houses in the heart of old Rye, and in later brickwork. There are letter-boxes with the word 'breven'; there is a *Flushing* inn; and quite a few local families have surnames derived from French and Flemish.

Minor grumblings and incidents were inevitable. At one stage immigration had to be halted because there was no more accommodation, and no more work. And of course there had to be one sharp dealer whose activities caused bad feeling towards others of his more innocent compatriots. Cornelys Shier bought up all available candles and employed other refugees to make more, establishing such a monopoly that if you refused to buy from him at his named price you risked spending your winter evenings in darkness. A formal complaint had to be made to the Lord Warden of the Cinque Ports before a stop could be put to this.

The storm which robbed New Romney of its river was for some centuries a blessing to Rye. The diverted Rother brought trade to the foot of her cliff, and the shipyards could launch reasonably large vessels; until, gradually, the inning of the marshes and the accumulation of silt in the bay and the river began to threaten this port, too. Rye Bay contracted. In the early nineteenth century it was still possible for an artist to sketch a scene showing water across the fields now known, for that reason, as the Town Salts. But after that the decline was rapid, and by the end of the century Rye was over two miles from the sea. To keep the narrow entrance of the Rother open, the harbour walls had to be strengthened and the encroaching shingle to be constantly fought back with a succession of huge groynes.

Rye is stranded. But how much better to suffer this fate rather than the fate of those towns which, remaining on the sea, have exploded out of all recognition.

A revenant from earlier centuries finding himself in Brighton, Shoreham or Hastings – above all, in London – might find difficulty in recognising more than a few thoroughfares, and even more difficulty in identifying specific buildings. In Rye he might be startled by some shop fronts and the emergence of so many tea-shoppes; but he would find that the steepness of the small hill and the compactness of its old housing has prevented too much extraneous building. Outside the town the housing estates have spread, and Cinque Ports Street is an untidy muddle, but within the boundary of the old wall the heart of the town seems unlikely to thrombose; though, as A. G. Bradley wrote in 1917, 'there is no protection against superfluous vandalism in this country, and in all probability never will be'.

I was born in Rye, in a house in Eagle Road, at the end of which my grandfather worked for a local contractor in a carpenter's shop. The smell of wood as a saw goes through it, or as it stands fresh and clean in the corner of a timber store, is still as evocative and intoxicating to me as Proust's madeleine. Taken away when I was too young to protest, I came back year after year on holiday until, after the Second World War, I was able to settle in the town for several years.

'Our soul is, above half of it, earth and stone in its affections and distempers' wrote Jeremy Taylor. Add some good Sussex timber, and I'll agree with him.

Each time I arrived on holiday the first imperative was to go out, to make a quick but thorough inspection of the town and make sure nothing terrible had happened: no house pulled down, no change in the names of familiar shopkeepers, no new horror on any skyline. Once the tour had been satisfactorily completed, the town took hold once more. This was the goal of all those months in exile, hoarding pennies and sixpences, poring over magic names in railway timetables, which I can recite to this day without any need of verification: Rye, Winchelsea, Snailham, Doleham, Three Oaks and Guestling, Ore, and Hastings.

In those days time was too precious to allow further exploration outside the town. I simply walked round and round

Rye. In a trance? If so, I must subconsciously have recorded a multitude of sights and sounds, for in dreams they can be summoned up even now. At least in dreams one is not jostled off the pavements or trapped between holidaymakers with cameras and groups of ladies swapping lurid instalments of their serial ailments outside the doctor's surgery. In the past it was painters and not photographers who blocked the way. Henry James saw many a party of them supervised by slouch-hatted gentlemen of whom he wrote:

> Leading a train of English and American lady
> pupils, they distribute their disciples at
> selected points, where the master going his
> rounds from hour to hour, reminds you of
> nothing so much as a busy *chef* with many
> saucepans on the stove and periodically
> lifting their covers for a sniff and a stir.
> There are ancient doorsteps which are used
> for their convenience of view and where the
> fond proprietor going and coming has to pick
> his way over paraphernalia, or to take
> flying leaps over industry and genius.

Which of us would not wish to have seen Henry James's bulky figure taking flying leaps over those painters and easels?

Any perambulation of the town should begin, obviously, at its remaining entrance gateway. The Landgate, with its great drum towers, is part of the fortifications authorised by Edward III. Bereft of its drawbridge and portcullis, it has been consoled by the insertion of a clock into its arch, a memorial to Victoria's Prince Consort.

Once within, past what was once the smithy, the eye is drawn by the great expanse of the levels, stretching away to Romney Marsh, with Dungeness atomic power station humped up on the tip of its promontory, and the hills leading on to Folkestone and Dover away in the east. And below, against a dazzle of river or tilted up on the mud along the Fishmarket, are the town's remaining fishing boats.

East Street, turning up beside the lovely bow window of the apothecary's shop, contains some stately houses and tempting little alleys dodging down towards that marshland view again. It also has, immediately opposite the vicarage, an inn called the *Union*. When I read of the wonderful talk in the *Tabard* of bygone days, or in the *Mermaid* (the London establishment, not the one just round the corner here in Rye), I sniff sceptically. Meaning no disrespect to the present tenant, I would wish the name of the late George Carruthers to go on record as the greatest and most stimulating landlord that ever was. Teetotal, grave in manner and slow of movement, he ran his premises and his customers largely by means of an expressively raised eyebrow, which somehow, while keeping the noise down, encouraged the most splendid conversation from a regular congregation of fishermen, shopkeepers, golfers, writers, musicians, retired army officers, a doctor, a dentist, a couple of peers of the realm. When I mentioned George years later to a Suffolk friend who had visited Rye, he recalled him at once: 'That landlord whose trousers kept his armpits up'. One of my own happier memories is of the evening I found the vicar in the bar, and made some flippant remark about dens of ill repute. 'No', said he rather solemnly, 'I will say that this is the best-run establishment of its kind in the town'. To which George, placing his two large hands flat on the counter, replied with equal solemnity: 'I can say the same about the vicarage, sir'.

History is not just a matter of remote kings, ancient wars and picturesque buildings. Living history rests as much on George Carruthers and his like – if ever there were his like again – as on the statesmen and soldiers and architects with their marble memorials and blue plaques.

Higher up, on the turn of the hill, is the *Flushing*. It was once an inn, and James Breads, the butcher of Rye who murdered a man he mistakenly thought to be the Mayor, against whom he had a grudge, was allowed to stop for a last drink there on his way to execution; but it ceased to be so in 1750, when an entry in the records of Brewster Sessions curtly declares the landlord 'broke'. The place is now a hotel and restaurant, with one room displaying a colourful sixteenth-century mural discovered in 1905 during renovations.

Pump Street is part of the cobbled unity of Church Square, opening out on to a wide slope beside the Ypres Tower. Henry III had exempted the Barons of Rye from paying him any of the revenues owed to him if they would guarantee instead to utilise the money on repairs to the sea walls, against flooding or enemy invasion of his realm. In 1249 he commanded the restoration of the castle at Hastings and, from any funds left over, the building of a new castle at Rye. During a period of municipal penury, this small keep was sold off in 1430 to a John de Ipres, after which it become known as the Ypres Tower. Local historians have bickered happily for years over these dates, some claiming that the tower was in fact built in 1135 by a Norman earl of Kent, William de Ypres, though there is no other reliable record of this nobleman. Either way, the dour old building has served faithfully as a watchtower, a shelter for townspeople during French raids, a prison, a mortuary, and is now an excellent museum.

The garden below is called the Gungarden or, by a few older people, the Battery. This may baffle the modern visitor. At one time the terrace housed a battery of guns covering the harbour approaches, and some old cannon were mounted decoratively there before the First World War. Between that war and the next there were a couple of 1914–18 field guns. All were removed at the outbreak of the Second World War so that the Nazis should have no excuse for bombing Rye as a supposed fortification. Not that they needed excuses: once the war began in earnest, Rye was bombed several times, destroying houses and the old museum adjoining the Ypres Tower, knocking the tower's roof off, and obliterating Henry James's old garden room at Lamb House. Then, in the closing stages of the war, the V.1 flying bomb offensive put the town right in 'doodle-bug alley'.

Watchbell Street, leading out of Church Square, housed a warning device older than air raid sirens. There are records of payments for wooden supports and steps to the bell, and for frequent renewal of the bell-rope, which must have been worn out by excessive use. No longer shaken by sea or air attacks, the street has always seemed to me much more gracious than the over-praised Mermaid Street.

St Mary's church has a churchyard decked with trees and flowering shrubs which nearly disappeared about 20 years ago, when misguided councillors proposed to uproot the lot, together with the gravestones, to facilitate mowing the grass. After a public meeting as stormy and abusive as any in Rye's lively history, the project was halted. The ramifications of the conflict could make a novel of English small-town life beside which *Clochemerle* would be pallid stuff.

It was the custom of the freemen to meet by an old cross in the churchyard and there elect their mayor. If he rejected the nomination, then 'the whole commons together shall go beat down his chief tenement'. Perhaps local government would be of a higher standard and freer from financial and other scandals if we revived this idea of electing to high office only men who have to be threatened into serving rather than those who hasten to put forward their own claim.

The north door and north window of the church, and its Elizabethan clock, stare straight down Lion Street into the busy shopping centre of the town. On each side of the clock is a quarter-boy, hammer poised to strike a bell. It was discovered some time ago that the boys were in fact a boy and girl, whereupon their sashes were repainted pink and blue.

Only recently it was found necessary to replace the wooden originals with fibre-glass facsimiles.

An American teacher once marshalled a group of school-girls on an educational trip across Lion Street, below the clock. It was 15 minutes past the hour. The quarter-boys struck one stroke each. 'Is that all?' asked a disappointed pupil. The teacher assured her brightly that they would come back on the hour, 'because absolutely *everything* happens on the hour'. It was typical of the stony-hearted passing Ryers (pronounced Royers) that not one told the poor lady that absolutely *nothing* happens on the hour, apart from the sound of the bell within the tower: the quarter-boys do not strike.

Inside, a long pendulum swings right down into the body of the church. Early in this century, when repairs were carried out for the first time in many generations, it was discovered that this heavy pendulum marking the seconds above the heads of the congregation was hanging from just one rusty nail.

The Burne-Jones and William Morris window was their last collaboration. Another window is that to the memory of Edward, brother of Alice Liddell, the original Alice in Wonderland. And there are windows to two Bensons: Edward White Benson, Archbishop of Canterbury, and his son A. C. Benson. Into the Nativity scene in the Archbishop's window the donor, his son E. F. Benson, has introduced his own dog among the shepherds, and a picture of himself in his robes as Mayor of Rye.

Benson lived in Lamb House for many years until his death in 1940. It was not an untimely death: he would have been saddened by the bombing, so soon after, of the garden room in which he had written so many books. Among them were the novels about Miss Mapp, the maliciously inquisitive lady who looked down West Street and along the cobbles towards the church, misinterpreted most of what she saw, and stirred

up continual intrigue in the very thinly disguised town of
'Tilling'.

Lamb House is named after the Lamb family, who for many
generations dominated Rye. It was nothing for one Lamb to
be mayor and his two sons to be jurats and magistrates at the
same time. Attempts to unseat them included a ruse in 1825
when the freemen met early and surreptitiously at the
churchyard cross, elected their own mayor instead of waiting
meekly for the Lamb nominee, and then took over the Guild-
hall and barricaded themselves in, carrying on the civic administration for six weeks in the teeth of the Lamb faction's
counter-claims. Eventually the Lambs had them ejected and
continued as the major power in the community until 1864,
when their remaining influence died with the death of Dr
Lamb, Rector of Iden, Playden and East Guldeford, and five
times mayor. The standard of this Tory parson's dealings with
his fellow citizens is demonstrated in his answer to petitioners
who appeared on one occasion before the Town Council:
'Gentlemen, we have entertained your petition, and . . . hee-
hee-hee . . . it has very much entertained us'.

It is, however, not with this local family that most people
associate Lamb House, but with an Anglophile American
who 'marked it for my own two years ago' and came to live
here in 1897.

> It is the very calmest and yet cheerfullest
> that I could have dreamed – *in* the little old,
> cobble-stoned, grass-grown, red-roofed town,
> on the summit of its mildly pyramidal hill
> and close to its noble old church– the chimes
> of which will sound sweet in my goodly old
> red-walled garden.

Henry James spent most of his summers and several winters
here until his death in 1916, visited by American friends and
relations, by Belloc, Chesterton and H. G. Wells, and by a

number of younger writers under his orotund spell. Some older Ryers remember yet the boom of his voice through the open window of the garden room when, in later years, he took to dictating his novels to an amanuensis.

*   *   *

One excursion I could be persuaded to make out of these haunted streets was to Camber. Today there is a huge holiday camp there, with rows of shacks and bungalows, and a constant stream of traffic in from East Guldeford. In the 1920s and 1930s a few wooden huts clung to the sand dunes, and not many people took the bus to the end where the camp and shops and chalets now stand : there was a much more enjoyable means of transport.

Below the bridge spanning the Rother at Rye was the station for the Rye and Camber Tram. Drawn in Henry James's day by a steam locomotive, it later acquired a small petrol engine whose chug-chug struck two distinctive echoes – one from a house it passed on the way to Camber, one from the cliff below the Ypres Tower on its return journey. I hear them still.

The first stop was at a tin-roofed station near the golf course. Henry James once accompanied E. F. Benson to the golf club, but found himself unable to rate golf very high among intellectual pursuits. 'Some beflagged jampots, I understand, my dear Fred, let into the soil at long but varying distances. A swoop, a swing, a flourish of steel, a dormy'.

Beyond was Camber Sands station, and a walk across sand or, sometimes, cracked mud-flats; and sometimes, then, there were higher tides than now and it was necessary to make long detours about inlets reaching almost up to the tramway embankment.

One day in 1973 the *Brighton Evening Argus* saw fit to report that a fisherman had actually caught a mackerel. *One* mackerel: this was newsworthy ? At Camber in the 1930s one did not even trouble to go out fishing for mackerel. Keddle nets were hung between poles at low tide, and when the water had flowed and ebbed again, thousands of them would be trapped for the taking. Any boy who helped to load the fish from the nets into the carts would be allowed to help himself to as many as he could carry.

Past Broomhill the coast road runs unnoticeably into Kent. The Kent Ditch, twisting down from the marsh in a series of jerky dog-legs, seems a purely arbitrary boundary. Walland, Denge and Romney Marshes are all intrinsically one with East Guldeford Level – the fifth continent of the world, according to Tom Ingoldsby and his creator, R. H. Barham.

The Kent Ditch joins the Rother below Northiam, a mile and a half east of Bodiam bridge, and for a while they keep company as divider of the counties. The river curves out of Wittersham Levels to join the Royal Military Canal. Crossing the canal, the ditch goes its own way. The Royal Military Canal and its parallel road were part of the defences ordered by Pitt against the Napoleonic invasion threat. Cobbett marvelled that 'those armies who had so often crossed the Rhine and the Danube were to be kept back by a canal, made by Pitt, thirty feet wide at the most!'

At Iden Lock, barracks were built for 30 soldiers, with an adjoining house for officers.

In Saxon times Iden and its neighbours, Peasmarsh, Beckley, Playden, Rye Foreign, Broomhill and East Guldeford, came into the hundred of Goldspur, and Iden and Playden formed the tithing of Hope. It was numbered among Earl Godwin's many possessions, but after the Conquest was presented, along with Hastings castle, to William's kinsman, Count Eu. By the time of Edward ii it belonged to one Nicholas de la Beche, who featured in a rather strange incident: having assisted two other knights to drag the king out of bed on Easter Monday in time to get to Mass, he shared in a grateful gift of £20.

All Saints' once had, like most churches of its time, a stone altar, but Edward vi commanded that all such should be discarded in favour of wooden tables. At Iden the stone slab was set in the ground by the south door so that the congregation should walk over it and thereby display their contempt for Roman Catholic beliefs.

There was once a castellated mansion here in the middle of an artificial lake, Iden Mote, which became the home of Sir John Scott, a fifteenth-century Lord Warden of the Cinque Ports. The Scotts lived here for many generations and were still in residence during the reign of Charles ii. Then they died out, leaving only their insignia on the tower of the church which Sir John's son had extended, and echoes in the farms called Baron's Grange and Moat Farm.

The oldest remaining house in the parish is Oxenbridge, propped up, restored and re-plastered many a time since its origin in the fourteenth century. It is probably called after the Oxnebregge or Oxenbridge family, whom we shall meet along the road in Brede.

Iden looks towards the marsh and sea on one side, towards the last furrows of the Weald on the other. It is a milder, less tempestuous Wild here, with neither the rolling breakers of the Downs nor quite the tangled secrecy of the deeper woods; more domesticated, with shallower and gentler ridges and flurries of land, abruptly steep at moments then apologetically smoothing out. High hedges twist some lanes into steep channels, chequered by sunlight through over-arching trees. At times it is impossible not to agree with Chesterton that before the Romans came to Rye or out to Severn strode, some rolling English drunkard, or more likely some Celtic drunkard, was responsible for these reeling, rolling, timeless and aimless roads. Then a more graceful curve of highway emerges from the woods to carry one on into long, straggling villages where white weather-boarding sets off brickwork and the glow of tile-hung frontages and tiled roofs. Everything looks newly washed, newly painted.

A thrush on a rose-hung fence . . . and butterflies, though not as many as when I was a boy.

At Peasmarsh the *Cock* tavern teeters on the rim of a swooping hill. The village was the birthplace in 1706 of William Pattison, the style of whose verse and the wretchedness of whose death led to his becoming known as the Chatterton of Sussex. With the aid of a generous patron he was sent away to school and on to Cambridge, where he quarrelled with his tutors and left just in time to avoid being sent down. Like many young writers with high hopes of fame and fortune, he sought congenial company in London; and after sleeping rough and coming close to starvation was befriended by Curll, the well-known bookseller. He died, before his twenty-first birthday, of smallpox.

The Norman church takes some finding, being set far on the other side of Peasmarsh Place, looking down on the placid valley of the Tillingham and across to Udimore.

In *The Four Men* Belloc recited many a litany of names whose sheer sound and personal resonances entranced him: Graffham and Cocking, Didling and Harting, Wolstonbury above New Timber and Highden and Rackham beyond and under Duncton the Garden of Eden. For some of us the most resonant names are here, within a small compass: Leasam and Marley, Cock Marling and Starvecrow, Gilly Wood, Conster, and sweet Doucegrove.

And over yonder is Glasseye Farm, and close to it Beckley Furnace.

The manor of Beckley itself was supposedly bequeathed by Alfred the Great to a favoured relative, but there may be some confusion with the Oxfordshire Beckley. Its church cap is a distinctive one, a reference point from all the lanes and rises in the neighbourhood, and there is an inviting lychgate – though perhaps 'inviting' is the wrong word for those of us who are in no great hurry to lie in our coffin below its shade. There is a tradition that FitzUrse, one of the assassins of Thomas à Becket, rode this far from Canterbury in search of sanctuary. Whether no intervening church would take him in, or whether he had relatives in the district who might be expected to help him, it is impossible to say. This is a long way from the scene of the murder. But then, he had farther yet to go: in the end, as far as the Holy Land, where he died as a penitent Crusader.

Beckley Furnace was noted for its production of large cannon. Today it is hard to believe, in this secluded, drowsy corner. But guns were made for the Cromwellians during the Civil War. When the iron industry was drawn away towards the coalfields, local craftsmen turned their hands to brasswork.

Above the Rother is Northiam, in whose praise Michael Drayton wrote in his versified guide-book, *Poly-Olbion*:

> O rare Norgem, thou dost far exceed
> Beckley, Peasemarsh, Udimore and Brede.

Until comparatively recently Northiam and Bodiam were Norgem and Bodgem in local dialect.

The road in from Beckley passes Brickwall, whose black and white half-timbered façade looks too regular and symmetrical to be genuine. It was in fact built in the sixteenth century by a family of Rye shipbuilders, and has been added to from time to time without altering its basic character. It soon came into the hands of the Frewens, who provided the parish with a large number of its rectors until the estate and the living were sold after the First World War. John Frewen, incumbent for 45 years, favoured Puritan doctrines and named his sons Accepted and Thankful. In spite of this, Accepted preferred Laud's liturgical views and the Royalist cause, and had to flee the country after Charles's defeat. His estates were confiscated, but returned after the Restoration, and he became Archbishop of York. There is a well-stocked Frewen mausoleum in Northiam church; but Accepted is buried in his minster at York.

In this century Brickwall became a school. Its interior is well cared for, and there is a fine staircase added by the Frewens. Also there is a pair of high-heeled shoes, left behind in 1573 by Queen Elizabeth. Possibly she kicked them off while enjoying an al fresco meal under the mighty oak tree on the village green, known ever since as Elizabeth's Oak. The food was brought out to her from the Hayes Hotel, which is much older than it looks. Elizabeth then went on to Rye for a formal reception by the mayor and jurats and, it is recorded, another outdoor meal. It must have been a balmy summer that year.

The ironstone church is a mixture of Early English, Decorated and Perpendicular, but with a Norman tower to which were added a turret in the fifteenth century and a spire in the sixteenth, made still loftier in the nineteenth.

Set back from the far end of the long, winding village is Great Dixter, another half-timbered manor house, this one about a hundred years older than Brickwall. It has been carefully restored, and enlarged by the incorporation of a similar house moved here bodily from Kent. The gardens were laid out by Sir Edward Lutyens in 1911. Noted for their clematis, they now operate as commercial nursery gardens without losing any of the original atmosphere.

Where the road downhill from Northiam is about to cross the Rother, the Kent Ditch and the Kentish border all at one time, there is an assemblage of old railway stock where Northiam station once flourished. This was once on the line of the Rother Valley Light Railway which ran from Robertsbridge to Tenterden, extended to Headcorn in 1905 and rechristened the Kent and East Sussex Railway. It was always a lovably eccentric, unreliable railway, and provided the inspiration for many of Rowland Emett's cartoons. Shortly

245

before its closure I seem to recall a delightful poem about it in *Punch*, garnished by some Emett drawings.

In his splendid book on Kent, Marcus Crouch remarks that 'Stories of the expedients adopted by driver and guard to keep up steam are no doubt enriched by exaggeration'. I am not so sure. Several older people of my acquaintance, not given to fantasy, have hilarious but convincing tales of near disaster. Official records are enough in themselves. The engine *Bodiam*, bought for the line in 1901 for £650, of which £500 was loaned by Barclays Bank on the understanding that a plaque would be fixed to the engine testifying to their generosity, had an alarming record before going into service here. It was once derailed at Victoria; ran into the back of a train near Battersea; and demolished a set of buffers at London Bridge. In its later years it went for a while into semi-retirement at Brighton, but was recalled in 1961 for the sad ceremony of hauling the last train from Tenterden to Robertsbridge. Yet when it was bought in 1964 and offered on permanent loan by two benefactors to the preservation society by then operating, the price they had to pay had gone up to £750.

In the early part of the century, before the river authority raised and strengthened the banks, flooding of the levels was not uncommon. Among their other duties the train drivers had to assess weather conditions before setting out from one station to the next. Shortly before Christmas 1910 there was especially heavy rainfall, and the Rother burst its banks. A train from Robertsbridge reached Bodiam to find water almost level with the top of the embankment. The driver decided to press on to Northiam, but the floods continued to rise above the axles of the locomotive. The train came to a halt, and passengers had to be rescued by boats and punts from Bodiam, taking only light hand luggage and returning when the water had subsided to salvage their heavier cases.

The Tenterden Railway Company is another group of

enthusiasts dedicated to the restoration and maintenance of a stretch of line. Volunteers work to clear the track between Tenterden and Bodiam, paint signal-boxes and stations, and get old engines back into shape. The full length between Robertsbridge and Headcorn will never be operated again – British Rail have removed large sections of the track – but experimental trains have been run on the existing metals, and played their part in some film and television episodes. Old *Bodiam* herself, who starred in 1947 in the film of *Joanna Godden*, made a comeback in 1973 in a new version of *Dracula;* and Bodiam station was painted and smartened up for scenes in a television series.

On Sunday 3 February 1974, after lengthy negotiations resulting in a Light Railway Transfer Order, passengers once more travelled between Tenterden and Rolvenden and, like pioneers pressing ever westward, the new Company hopes eventually to carry weekend and holiday visitors into Sussex and once more to Bodiam. Not only is there no better way of seeing the changing moods of the Rother valley : there is no other way at all, since no road runs along it and the river no longer carries the small boats in which it was possible, once upon a time, to travel unhurriedly from the Star Lock to Bodiam.

Even if fully restored, the railway could unfortunately never reclaim its old nickname, 'the Hoppers' Line'. During the brief picking season it used to be crammed with East Enders on their way to the hop gardens which cling to every slope here. This was their annual holiday, and one on which they relied for a much-needed addition to their income. Today the hops are plucked from the bine by machinery, with perhaps a few locals lending a hand. And even then, there is a danger of many gardens being closed down: while growers puzzle out E.E.C. demands for the introduction of seedless hops and the elimination of the English male plant, many brewers are importing mash from the Continent and turning away from their old traditions. They say it won't affect the taste or quality of the beer; but they have said that before, at each stage of so-called rationalisation and at each big takeover – and those of us with palates in good working order know the truth.

The white caps of too many oast houses are now grey and neglected. Others, smartly repainted, turn above old roundels which have been fitted with windows and converted into very desirable residences. There are those who deplore this fashion for spruced-up oast houses. Far better, surely, that their graceful shape should be preserved like this rather than left to crumble into ruin. There is a very fetching group in Ewhurst, beside the equally desirable Preacher's House.

Ewhurst church spire looks odd from any angle. One blinks, looks away, and looks again, alarmed by some possible trick of the eyesight. It appears to bulge on one side, and to topple slowly towards the other. This is the result of a reconstruction in 1792 after the spire had been struck by lightning. The very first entry in the church register, opened in the first year of the reign of Elizabeth I, is a sad one:

Nicholas Scott had two children the one was
christened at home the 26th day of Novr. and
buried the same day the other was baptised
the same day and named also John.

Two weeks later we learn that this John also died.

In the church is a fourteenth-century font of Sussex marble. There is a small brass from 1520, and some modern stained glass in the clerestory. Outside, in the west buttress of the south wall, are traces of a mass clock: when a stick was inserted into one of the holes it provided a sundial from which the priest could read the time for mass.

From this ridge we look straight down on Bodiam castle, one of the great showpieces of the county, a fairy-tale picture, the archetype of all moated castles from which spotless knights gallop out in search of dragon-pestered maidens. Its setting was once enhanced by a profusion of water lilies on the moat, but recently these have had to be cut back, and it may be some time before they are allowed to spread so luxuriantly again.

The builder of the castle was Sir Edward Dalyngruge, who was very far from being a pure and chivalrous knight. He allied himself with the notorious Edward Knollys in France, and with other freebooters they roamed the countryside indulging in what its adherents might call guerrilla warfare but was in fact ruthless banditry. They killed, robbed, and made a speciality of abducting and holding to ransom widows and defenceless young women of property. It is hardly surprising that on his return to England, loaded with booty, Dalyngruge should take steps to protect himself against French retaliation. Having married the heiress to a property at Bodiam, he began in 1386 to build himself a castle on the site.

The curtain-walled fortress is 160 feet square, its thick circular towers 70 feet high. The imposing gatehouse still has an intact iron portcullis, and a great nail-studded door. Around the courtyard, on to which the living rooms of the castle faced, there are relics of a chapel, the kitchens, and other features.

After all Sir Edward's troubles, he was never attacked. His position certainly seemed vulnerable, for in those days the Rother opened out here into a broad estuary, and royal approval of the fortifications was granted the more readily because of the need to repel probable invaders. But although the French repeatedly hammered Hastings, Rye and Winchelsea they never ventured as far as Bodiam.

Sir Edward left the castle to his son, and then it passed to the old Sussex family of the Lewknors. In none of the many later conflicts within and without the realm did it play any significant part, though in 1643 the Parliamentarians took the precaution of dismantling it. Jack Fuller saved it from complete decay, and finally it was restored and bequeathed to the National Trust by Lord Curzon of Kedleston in 1926.

Bodiam village is little more than a tiny adjunct to the castle, providing teas and postage stamps to its visitors. There is still some work for students in the extensive Guinness hop gardens, but rumour has it that they, too, will soon be redundant. Perhaps the main excitement in the village is the annual pancake race for women every Shrove Tuesday.

Where the road out of Bodiam emerges on to the A.229, a few hundred yards north and just within Sussex is Great Wigsell. Another iron-master's house, it looks from the road not unlike another Bateman's. It was once the home of the Culpepers and more recently of Lord Milner who, like them, is buried at Salehurst.

Turning left rather than right, we come down the hill into a gently descending village street which at any time of year and in any weather is a joy to behold. Sedlescombe's houses are set well back on one side, and protected on the other by a village green and a quieter slip road – though not so quiet when cars begin to crowd up towards the *Queen's Head*, an old coaching inn which dates back before 1600. The bar has a Sussex fire-back from 1754.

Until recent years the pump on the green was the village's only water supply. It is still a spot where locals tend to slow their pace, linger, and chat.

Set in delightful gardens across the head of the street is Brickwall, once the home of the Farndens, seventeenth-century iron-masters. Others in the same trade were the Bishop family, who have an iron memorial slab in the church.

The chestnut trees to the west of the churchyard are known to have been established here well before the reign of Charles I.

In 1876, during the digging of a drain opposite the village school, a hoard of silver coins were unearthed. They proved to have been minted in the time of Edward the Confessor, and it is thought they must have been meant as payment for Harold's troops. Many Saxons fled this way after the defeat: perhaps someone took charge of the war chest and then had to bury it; or it may have been left here for safety's sake as Harold marched towards Senlac for the confrontation.

On a hill above Sedlescombe is one of the Pestalozzi children's villages, named after the Swiss educational reformer. This community in Oaklands Park was established in 1958, and it was regarded as a happy omen that the flower-beds should be so well stocked with Peace roses.

The aim of these settlements is to provide children from all over the world with a wide education which will enable them to go back to their own countries equipped to serve their own people. Although the Trust is registered as a charity and depends entirely on voluntary subscriptions it is not a charitable institution in the usual sense. Its aid is complementary to the relief of hunger and poverty in under-developed or war-torn countries. The children are taught essential skills and also, in this international atmosphere, share ideas and ideals with those of other races and creeds.

Pupils generally stay here between the ages of 11 and 18. With the help of teaching machines, they usually find they can master English well enough in their first three months to cope with more advanced education. The emphasis is on the practical. There is a farm, and a carpenter's shop. The boys do much of the repair and redecorating work in the village, and in an emergency have been able to build complete new houses. Although the Pestalozzi foundation is in no way a refugee organisation, it did react quickly when children were scattered from Vietnam and, above all, when Tibetan children came over after the Chinese invasion. Unlike most of their friends, these will probably never be able to go back to their own lands.

Girls tend to choose weaving and pottery as their practical

subjects. Coaches take some children to local technical schools or, in the case of the few under-elevens who for various reasons have been accepted, into the village to local primary schools. In return, a number of bricklayers' apprentices are admitted into the village to practise their craft, an arrangement which suits both sides very well.

There are separate houses for different nationalities where they can wear their own costume and speak their own language; but there is also a communal hall where they are encouraged to meet. The setting is so magnificent, the overall atmosphere so friendly, that one can only hope that on return to their own countries the boys and girls will not feel too homesick for Sedlescombe.

From Brickwall a lurching, winding road has difficulty making up its mind on the best route to Broad Oak or Brede. One spur runs close beside Powdermill Reservoir, recalling a sequence of disasters in the parish. After closure of an iron furnace here, its site was reconstituted as a factory for producing gunpowder during the Napoleonic wars. Three times it blew up, killing most of its workers.

In the late fifteenth century Sir Thomas Oxenbridge began to build himself a house above the River Brede. Continued by Sir Goddard Oxenbridge, it was first called Forde Place and then Brede Place. Various additions, including a little chapel, were made over the years, and in due course the mansion acquired a ghost – very much in evidence when, for some years unoccupied, the house was used as a storehouse for contraband.

The ghost was identified as that of Sir Goddard. He had the reputation of being both a giant – another name for Brede Place has been 'The Giant's House' – and a child-eater. His supper was not complete without one whole infant. In desperation the children of the neighbourhood concocted a sleeping draught from hops and managed to get it to his table. When he was unconscious, they sawed him in two. Sir

Goddard nevertheless lies decorously enough in Brede church; unlike his kinsman Sir Robert, whose figure in a brass seems to have been gnawed away by someone as greedy as the ogre.

Later occupants of Brede Place included Stephen Crane, the American author of *The Red Badge of Courage*, who admitted that he needed all his courage to cope with strange ghostly phenomena; and Clare Sheridan, who wrote about it in *My Crowded Sanctuary*, and some of whose sculptures are still to be found there and in St George's church. It was while staying in the house that J. M. Barrie heard the story of a pirate turned parson, and invented Captain Hook. Was it here or elsewhere, one wonders, that Russell Thorndike also heard the story and created Doctor Syn?

In addition to the Oxenbridge chantry, the church has a massive, intricately carved chest, an old poor-box, a good modern pulpit, and, of all incongruous things, Jonathan Swift's cradle.

Across the River Brede is Westfield, which I fear I have never regarded as anything more than a stop on one of the bus routes from Hastings to Rye. The alternative route leads through Guestling, which offers from the top of White Hart Hill on a clear day the most dizzying panorama of Pett Level, Rye Bay, the ridge to Winchelsea, and, tiny but unmistakable on the edge of the farther foothills, Rye.

Guestling is hardly a village: more a scattering of amiable neighbours on a cluster of hummocks like small, long-overgrown mine workings. In a house near the railway halt of Three Oaks and Guestling was born Gregory Martin, translator of the Douai version of the Bible.

The tower of Fairlight is a stumpy silhouette against the seaward sky. A little way below, Pett asserts itself with a jaunty spire. 'Which is the way to Brede?' was the question, asked by unwary strangers, to which the locals had several well-rehearsed, ribald responses. In this century, 'Which is the way to Pett?' is eagerly awaited as a corollary.

Down dives the road on to Pett Level, where the Military Canal from Hythe reaches its western extremity.

Most of this reclaimed marsh lies below sea level. The shingle bank for ever threatening to suffocate Rye Harbour is here a protector rather than enemy; but not a dependable one. In 1926 the sea burst through and flooded the level. Although the gap was filled in, it was obvious that sooner or later more ambitious defences would have to be constructed. It is the repeated irony of all such coastlines: while the water recedes from one port utterly reliant on it, only a few miles away it is slowly or savagely eroding land which would be well content without it.

During the Second World War it was calculated, and afterwards confirmed from German documents, that Hitler's invasion, Operation Sea-Lion, would be launched against this stretch of coast. Once again the sea wall was breached, this time deliberately, to flood about 1,000 acres. The level, like most of the shores and marshes of the south-east, became a prohibited area.

But while it was possible to forbid the English to visit their own coasts, and possible to plan effective defences against the Germans, it was not possible to ban other visitors, native or foreign. From the moment that this sheet of water appeared within the sea wall, broken only by slight irregularities in the ground to form islands, birds began to arrive by the dozen. Ducks and waders had found not just a holiday resort but a home, utterly undisturbed by human beings. Gulls, terns, mallards, lapwings – the word spread, and in they all came.

In 1944 the water was drained away, and the land reclaimed. It must have been a great blow to the wartime population. But by 1950 some of their scouts may have started sending out optimistic messages again. A major scheme for strengthening the wall with steel and concrete was put in hand, and a great deal of earth was dug out of four wide trenches in the level. These promptly filled with water; and promptly the birds began to flock back. Today there is a solid sea wall from Cliff End to Winchelsea Beach, with an accompanying road below, a walk along the top, and steps cut into it at intervals to give access to the shore. And there is a bird-watcher's paradise on the artificial lakes.

Winchelsea Beach is best avoided. It is a shingly, second-rate Camber, and if growth continues as at present I foresee an unhappy day when it crowds right in on Rye Harbour.

Above the level is Icklesham, marked by its windmill and by a strong-towered Norman church. Beyond, the ground descends again almost at once into the trough of the River Brede, and rises again to Udimore on the parallel ridge. Udimore reputedly owes its name to a mysterious message whispered in the ears of its church builders, who worked every day on one side of the duckpond only to find that every night their stones were shifted to the other side. 'Over the mere!' commanded the ethereal voices. The masons gave in, and completed Over-the-mere church on the specified side of the pond.

It was in Udimore that Edward I stayed with the Echynghams when supervising construction of the new Winchelsea he had decreed on its hilltop. And it was from a vantage point here that Queen Philippa looked across Icklesham ridge to Rye Bay, where her husband Edward III commanded his fleet against the Spaniards in 1350. As soon as they had landed after a great victory, Edward and his son, the Black Prince, rode with their knight full speed to Udimore, where, according to Froissart, 'they passed the night in revelling with the ladies, conversing of arms and armours'. Many ladies in many centuries have been resigned to such conversation: boastful military reminiscence cannot, for many of them, have come into the category of revelry.

From Udimore a road past Winchelsea's remote railway station climbs into Winchelsea through the old Land Gate. The Icklesham ridge sinks, rises, and leads into the town with-

out having to negotiate any such narrow arch. A third
remaining gate straddles the steep road in from Rye, on a bend
which has trapped many an incautious bus driver. Perched
beside this, the Strand Gate, is the house in which Ellen Terry
lived for many years before being tempted away to
Smallhythe.

In the early times of the Cinque Ports, Winchelsea was of
far greater consequence than its twin Ancient Town, Rye. This
Winchelsea, however, did not survive. Dangerously low-
lying, it was repeatedly damaged by storm, and in 1250 lost
half its houses. It risked losing a lot more when, in 1265, it
was the only Cinque Port to remain loyal to Simon de Montfort and offer refuge to his hard-pressed adherents. The king
himself came to break into this last stronghold and exact
retribution.

But having breached the walls, Edward I was wise enough
to see that these walls were essential to the defence of
England. Another natural catastrophe might mean the loss of
one of his frontier bastions. Rather than destroy it in vengeful
mood, he would rebuild it. Land was bought in the parish of
Icklesham, and on a sandstone plateau Edward personally
designed a new town on a grid pattern of squares, rectangles
and right-angled intersections, covering 90 acres within a
containing wall and four gateways.

He had acted just in time. The population had not been
fully evacuated to the new site when old Winchelsea was
swept away in that tempest of 1287 which wrenched the
Rother off course and, as the new Winchelsea struggled to
establish itself, gave new power to Rye.

A worthy church was planned on the hill, but either was
never finished or was devastated early on by French raiders,
for today there remain only a great chancel and accompanying fragments which may represent something half-completed
or half-demolished. The nine windows given by Lord Blane-
burgh after the First World War were designed by Douglas

Strachan in three groups as a general and personal war memorial, combined with a testimony to the enduring values of the countryside and the ideals for which men have suffered and striven.

Among the weighty tombs are those of the Alards. Gervase, a fourteenth-century Admiral of the Cinque Ports, was the first Englishman to be given the title of admiral.

This tomb is mentioned in *Denis Duval*, the novel which Thackeray left unfinished at his death. The characters who inspired the story are local, too. Near the church are remains of a friary: although the estate has been in private hands since Henry VIII dispossessed its monks, it is still called Greyfriars. In 1781 it was rented by two brothers, Joseph and George Weston, whose lavish hospitality and gentlemanly bearing made a great impression in the district. Then it was learned that all this display derived from their income as highwaymen, in particular from a rich haul they had made from the Bath and Bristol mail coach. They were identified and arrested in April 1782, escaped, but were recaptured and hanged at Tyburn.

Such a blend of apparent respectability and roguery seems characteristic of the whole coastal fraternity. My grandmother once told me about *her* grandmother swaying innocently to and fro in her rocking-chair while Revenue officers searched their Winchelsea house for smuggled goods, without success: the reason for their failure being that the mat beneath the rockers of her chair covered a crucial trap-door.

John Wesley preached his last outdoor sermon at Winchelsea in October 1790, under the great ash tree near the *New Inn*. On earlier visits he recorded in his diary that he 'found abundance of people willing to hear the good word' in Rye and Winchelsea, but lamented 'they will not part with the accursed thing smuggling, so I fear, with regard to these, our labour will be in vain . . . how large a Society would be here, could we but spare them in one thing'.

It must have been at the foot of the hill below the Strand Gate that John Galsworthy and Ford Madox Hueffer (later Ford Madox Ford) were, according to Hueffer, brought to a respectful halt by one of Henry James's more involved discourses. The result was an entanglement more than usually complex, even for the Master. He had brought his dachshund Maximilian out for the walk, allowing it a very long leash so that it could sniff about more freely. As they stood rooted to the spot, Maximilian began to weave in and out of the legs of Galsworthy and Hueffer, who did not dare to allow their attention to waver from the protracted disquisition. When at last James finished and walked on, the other two men had to fight their way out of the tightening coils of Maximilian's leash as he tried to follow. Hueffer never forgot the resulting fury, as the great man slammed his cane to the ground and denounced the playing of such tricks as an imbecility – 'an im ... be ... cility!'

The road to Rye runs very straight, with just one kink in it. Here, where it pulls into line with the canal, is a glimpse of castle before the bank obscures it. This old ruin, reached by footpath from the junction with the Rye Harbour road, is that of Camber castle. It is some distance from Camber, with the Rother in between, but the land on which it stands was once a promontory thrusting out across the estuary towards a promontory from Camber itself. There was a spell during which it was known, more appropriately, as Winchelsea castle: appropriate in every way, since the stones for its building came almost exclusively from the dismembered religious houses of Winchelsea.

When Henry VIII had been excommunicated and was threatened by both France and Spain with stronger armies than he could readily muster, he concentrated on sea defences, and in 1539 allocated some of the wealth seized from the monasteries to the 'Device of the King for new Blockhouses or Bulwarks'. The three main strongholds were those of

Deal, Walmer and Sandown in Kent. Camber, a subsidiary fortress, follows the Tudor rose pattern so clearly preserved at Deal.

Through Elizabeth's time it remained a valuable sentry commanding the harbour entrance, but by the early 1640s was abandoned. The Mayor and Jurats of Rye were instructed to take away lead, timber and anything else they considered of value rather than let it fall into the hands of individual predators, and after handing the material over to the Committee of Sussex were granted a contribution towards their own fortifications. There was a volunteers' camp here at the end of the nineteenth century; and during the Second World War it shook to the roar of ack-ack guns during the worst of the flying-bomb campaign. Until recently it was possible to wander in and out of the gaps of its walls, over the uneven ground and rubble, and through the nettles; but at the time of writing, the wire installed to deter sheep has been augumented by further barriers and the warning that the building is unsafe for human as well as animal visitors.

With the contraction of the estuary and the isolation of the castle on the levels, the village of Rye Harbour has grown up beside the narrower river. Its only military installation is the dry-moated Martello tower. The two pubs have some martial echoes, though: the *Inkerman* and, right on the hard by the slipway, the *William the Conqueror*. There is always a bustle here. Fishing boats and small timber boats still go to and from Rye. There is a coastguard station on the far wall of the harbour; the sailing club takes possession at week-ends and during the holiday season; and there is an R.N.L.I. light rescue boat.

Once there was a full-size lifeboat. In such a small community, its crew represented a large proportion of available manpower, and bore the brunt of many hazardous operations from the lifeboat shed away across the shingle. During its years of service the station saved a total of 128 lives. On 15

November 1928, 17 men put out in a south-westerly gale in answer to a distress call. The *Mary Stanford*, the sixth boat to serve on the station, capsized, with the loss of all hands.

Within the little church, its roof like an inverted ship's hull, is a memorial tablet of Manx stone given by the people of the Isle of Man, birthplace of the Royal National Lifeboat Institution. In the churchyard the bodies of the crew, washed ashore, lie beneath a sad yet proud monument. To read the names on the individual plaques is to see what the disaster must have meant to certain local families.

There are times when the church itself seems in some danger as the gravel-pit workings draw closer and closer. The clutter of small factories, stores and abandoned junk between here and Rye is a monstrous eyesore. All that can be said in favour of this road is that from it you are offered the loveliest view of Rye other than that from the river itself.

A turn beside Rock Channel, on to the main road and over the bridge, with the windmill and the River Tillingham to the left, and we are on the Strand and back, full circle, in the town.

*   *   *

Coaches park here, and many visitors start their exploration at the foot of steep, cobbled Mermaid Street. Two of its most striking houses are associated with the Jeake family : a three-gabled, sixteenth-century one known as the Old Hospital after its service in that capacity during the Napoleonic wars; and one dated 1689, on the other side of the street, with a sign inset by the younger Samuel Jeake to record the astrological portents prevailing when he laid its foundation stone. The house survives in good shape, so presumably the stars were propitious. He had chosen his wife by similar calculations, married her when she was 13, and seems to have been very well content with the match.

But the first building most people think of when Rye is mentioned, and which may fittingly be the last we mention here, is the *Mermaid Inn*.

It has stood here since the fifteenth century, and both interior and exterior have suffered many vicissitudes; but despite a great deal of tampering and titivation, the face it presents to the street is a venerable one. Behind that long façade, which has at one time and another embraced neighbouring houses, are hidden a warren of passages, rooms large and small, twisting stairs and mysterious cellars. It has memories of many a smuggling venture. William Holloway, the town's major historian, was once told by a gentleman born in Rye in 1740 that he had personally seen known members of the Hawkhurst gang 'seated at the windows of this house, carousing and smoking their pipes, with their loaded pistols lying on the table before them, no magistrate daring to interfere with them'.

At some date not long after this the premises ceased to be a hostelry until, at the end of the last century, they became a licensed club and then once more a fully fledged inn.

In 1971 and 1972, overseas visitors represented such a high proportion of the guests that the *Mermaid* justifiably received one of the Queen's Awards to Industry. The country undoubtedly needs foreign currency – our political and financial leaders seem to have little interest in any other subject – so I suppose the apotheosis will come when every hotel in Rye, and then in Sussex, and ultimately throughout the entire country, is given over exclusively to foreign visitors, while the rest of us stay at home trying to work out why our taxes are still so high and our standard of life still so modest.

But in my time I, too, have lived in Arcady. The view from the footpath along the Tillingham has been obscured by a housing estate, the market is a shadow of its former self, the eccentric painter who soothingly played the piano all night in an attic beyond my grandmother's garden died long ago, and there is talk of doing away with the railway line, which means the end of that sudden, startling, unforgettable throb when a train from the marsh strikes the bridge across the Rother. But in memory all of it remains clear and real. The Rye of today and tomorrow will be just as clear and indestructible, in its changing moods, in the memories of another generation and generations far on, I trust, into and beyond another century.

Above the church clock which has worked unflaggingly since the days of the first Elizabeth, the inscription between the quarter-boys tells us not to repine:

For our time
is a very shadow
that passeth
away.

Bibliography

There must be many books, newspapers, letters and pamphlets, read at different times over many years, from which memory has selected material whose sources I cannot now identify. If anywhere in this book I have come close to quoting or misquoting anyone without due acknowledgment, I apologise most sincerely.

In more recent times I have learned much from more church and local guides, and local conversations, than I could possibly list here. The titles given below are of books which, quite apart from their value as reference material, I would recommend as being thoroughly readable in their own right.

Bradley, A. G., *An Old Gate of England* (Robert Scott, 1917)
Brentnall, Margaret, *The Cinque Ports and Romney Marsh* (John Gifford, 1972)
Carfax Publications, *Causeway* (Carfax, Horsham, 1971/72)
Carfax Publications, *History of West Sussex* (Carfax, Horsham, 1972/73)
Christian, Garth, *Ashdown Forest* (Society of Friends of Ashdown Forest, 1967)
Cooper, William, *Smuggling in Sussex* (Frank Graham, 1966)
Copper, Bob, *A Song for Every Season* (Heinemann, 1971)
Crouch, Marcus, *Detective in the Landscape in South East England* (Longmans, 1972)
Done, W. E. P., *Looking Back in Sussex* (Faber, 1953)
Evershed-Martin, Leslie, *The Impossible Theatre* (Phillimore, 1971)
Fleet, Charles, *Glimpses of our Sussex Ancestors* (Farncombe. Two vols., 1882/83)
Hales, Marianne, *Bygone Iden* (Adams & Son, 1950)

Holloway, William, *History of the Town and Port of Rye*
  (John Russell Smith, 1847)
Kaye-Smith, Sheila, *The Weald of Kent and Sussex*
  (Robert Hale, 1953)
Meynell, Esther, *Sussex* (Robert Hale, 1947)
Musgrave, Clifford, *Life in Brighton* (Faber, 1970)
Odell, Mary Theresa, *The Old Theatre, Worthing*
  (Geo. W. Jones, Aylesbury, 1938)
Odell, Mary Theresa, *Mr Trotter of Worthing and the Brighton
  Theatre* (Aldridge Bros., 1944)
Vidler, Leopold Amon, *A New History of Rye* (Combridges,
  1934)
Vine, P. A. L., *London's Lost Route to the Sea*
  (David and Charles, 1973)

Index

Italicized figures refer to Plate numbers.

Index

Index

Index